W9-DDJ-086

Stewards of God

Stewards of God

Milo Kauffman

HERALD PRESS
Scottdale, Pennsylvania
Kitchener, Ontario
1975

Library of Congress Cataloging in Publication Data

Kauffman, Milo, 1898-
    Stewards of God.

    Includes bibliographical references.
    1. Stewardship, Christian — Biblical teaching.
I. Title
BV772.K33   248'.6   74-13130
ISBN 0-8361-1747-6

TO MY WIFE, CLARA

Who through life has been my constant companion
in stewardship of the gospel, this book is affectionately
dedicated.

CONTENTS

PREFACE

Few things in nearly fifty years in the Christian ministry have been more meaningful and rewarding to me than the practice and promotion of Christian stewardship. The great promises of God in His Word to His faithful stewards are by no means idle words nor exaggerations. God is still waiting to open the windows of heaven and pour out His blessings.

Having passed the life-span of "threescore years and ten" I find myself constantly being the recipient of God's blessings for decisions, attitudes, and actions of the past fifty years. Sacrifices made, services rendered, tithes and offerings presented have been rewarded manifold. If through the writing of this book one person can be helped to experience the joy and blessings that I have received and that are certain to follow when faithful stewardship is practiced, the time and energy given in the preparation of this manuscript will be well spent.

Without the help of many people this book would not be possible. I am grateful to Herald Press for inviting me to submit the manuscript; to the Conrad Grebel Lectureship Committee for permitting me to use any material from my former book, *The Challenge of Christian Stewardship;* to

President Laban Peachey and to Hesston College for the encouragement given and for making it possible for me to give time to this work. I have appreciated the constant encouragement and suggestions given by my friend, Andrew Shelly. Wilbert Shenk, Executive Secretary of Mennonite Board of Missions, was also helpful in reading the manuscript and giving suggestions and criticisms.

Also, I wish to express my gratitude to those who sent me their testimonies or furnished other materials. There are others who read parts of the manuscript and offered suggestions. I offer special thanks to my daughter, Phyllis, for faithful work in typing the manuscript. To all who have helped in any way or who have given their encouragement I say a hearty "Thank you."

Several publishers kindly gave their consent to quote from books or publications. Acknowledgments have been made in footnotes or at the proper place.

Milo Kauffman

1

THE CHALLENGE OF CHRISTIAN STEWARDSHIP

What could be more thrilling or challenging than to be a steward of God in the 70s as we see the mighty moving of God's Spirit! His great purposes are steadily going forward, and we have the happy privilege of being His stewards in promoting these purposes. The Holy Spirit is moving mightily among many groups of people around the world. Young people of many nations are finding Jesus Christ by the thousands as the answer to their emptiness, their frustrations, and their needs.

A missionary in Africa declared that we are living in a time when more people are being added to the church than in any other period in history — thousands in Indonesia, in Africa, in Latin America, Taiwan, Korea, and elsewhere. Efforts are being made to get the written Word to all peoples of the world in the 70s.

God through the Prophet Joel said that in the latter days He would pour out His Spirit on all flesh (2:28). Jesus said that the good news of the kingdom shall be proclaimed to all men over the world, then will the end come (Mt. 24:14). We are seeing the Spirit of God being poured out and witnessing the good news of the kingdom being taken to all people. What exciting days to be stewards of God and have a part in the promotion of God's kingdom on earth! What a challenge to dedicate life and possessions for the ongoing program of God!

God's Sublime Plan for Man

God created man to be the dwelling place of His Spirit. He wanted man to be like Himself, possessing the qualities of freedom, holiness, love, and righteousness. He created man to be His steward, to share and to portray His glory, His joy, His peace, and His power. God purposed in the ages past to have in the earth a community of love and righteousness.

When man through self-will spurned God's love and disobeyed Him His purposes were not overthrown. He had a plan for man's reconciliation and redemption. His plan included the atonement at Calvary and the establishment of His church, Christ's body. It also included the heavenly kingdom prepared from the foundation of the world (Mt. 25:34).

God's plan for the reconciliation of the world included man's total restoration into the image of God. The people of God, the perfect community of love and righteousness, that God purposed in the beginning will become a reality. Sin, injustice, unbelief, immorality, and all that defiles will be cast out. All the scars resulting from man's sin will be removed. God's people will be holy as He is holy, merciful as He is merciful, and perfect as He is perfect. Perfectly they will share and portray His glory, His joy, and His love.

God's eternal plan included that we, His people, be co-workers with Him in the fulfillment of these purposes. He chose us before the foundation of the world and predestined us to be His children. He committed to us the ministry of reconciliation. We are stewards of the manifold grace of God. As stewards our primary concern is to help restore people to the image of God, to promote God's community of love and righteousness.

Some Concerns for God's Stewards

A number of things should deeply concern the stewards of God today. A majority of the people of the world remain unevangelized, yet as God's people we are stewards of the gospel. It is our task to make disciples of all nations. So many professing Christians are living selfishly and in defeat, falling far short of the image of God. We are stewards of God in perfecting the saints and bringing them to spiritual maturity. There are so many of the people of our world living in abject poverty, sickness, ignorance, superstition, and fear. We are God's stewards in ministering to them. As we neglect them we neglect our Lord.

Is it possible that we, the professed followers of the Lord, by selfishness and avarice, by our indifference and lack of compassion for the downtrodden, permit our Lord to live in the ghetto, in the slums and the dens of poverty? As we permit others to live in poverty and misery, are we not permitting the Lord thus to live? He dwells with His people. Jesus said, "As you neglect these you neglect me."

God wants His people to have eternal life. He wants them to grow in Christlikeness. But He also wants them to have food and clothing. He asks us to share and minister to their needs. He intended that the people of the earth share His riches. Unfortunately the gold and silver, the cattle, the rich resources that God intended for all men to share have fallen into the hands of a few who insist on using them selfishly or holding on to them, to the misery and degradation of the masses.

Is it fair for one family to have more food than they

can eat, more money than they can spend, more clothes than they can wear, and more houses than they can live in while other families have no food to eat, no money to spend, only rags to wear, and no roof over their heads? Christian stewardship demands that we share and that we teach others to share.

It is the right of everyone to have sufficient earthly goods for his needs. As men follow justice, exercise compassion, and practice Christian stewardship, the necessities of life will be provided for everyone. The covetousness and selfishness of man, his lack of a sense of stewardship, are responsible for the large areas of poverty in today's world.

Man's sin is his failure to be a good steward, refusal to use God's gifts for God's glory, and failure to live as an obedient creature under the sovereign will of his Creator. Man's will to be free has enslaved him. The prodigal's sin was not in wasting his inheritance. This was but a symptom of his strong desire to be free of his father's will and to be his own master. The true steward is concerned in doing the Father's will and in ministering to the welfare of his brothers.

The Christian steward must be interested in leading people from darkness into the marvelous light, in helping them grow in the image of the Son. He will be concerned also in lifting people from the ghettos, and in lifting them from poverty, releasing them from superstition and fear. The steward is a partner of God in helping people experience healing and wholeness spiritually, mentally, and physically. As stewards we employ all the resources given us by God to help people become the kind of persons God wants in His community of righteousness.

Why Have We Failed?

Why do the purposes of God go forward so slowly?

Why have so few people of the world been evangelized? Why has the church so failed in conforming to the image of Christ? Why must so many of the people of the world languish in poverty and suffering when God has entrusted the wealth of the world to mankind?

It is because man's eyes have been blinded by sin. He sees only dimly the great acts of God in the past. He fails to comprehend the great purposes of God for today and for tomorrow and the exalted place God wants His stewards to fill in the work of His kingdom. Consequently, man does not respond to God's grace with genuine gratitude and commitment. This also militates against a living faith, a faith that forsakes all and follows Him, a faith that seeks first the kingdom of God, a faith that gives generously of self and possessions.

Man lacks a proper concept of God the Creator and Redeemer. He has an inadequate concept of the great and benevolent purposes of God. He has a distorted view of himself as God's steward. These inadequate concepts militate against a dynamic stewardship and the fulfillment of God's purposes.

Another area of man's failure as a steward of God is in taking seriously his relationship to God's creation. God is concerned not only in the reconciliation and redemption of man, but also in the redemption of all His creation. God's concern for man includes His concern for man's habitation, his environment.

Western man has through industry and technology built an affluent society, but is choking from the fumes of automobiles and the smoke of industrial plants. He is in danger of being poisoned by the wastes being dumped into our rivers and lakes. He has ruined millions of acres of farming and grazing land by careless farming and mining in his greed for wealth. He has recklessly exploited the

15

forests, the minerals and rich resources of the earth, disregarding the welfare of future generations. If man is to survive on the planet earth he must quickly and earnestly respond to the challenge of stewardship of the earth.

Failure in rendering to God the tithes and offerings, unfaithfulness in the stewardship of possessions, has greatly impeded the spread of the gospel and the promotion of the kingdom of God. The greatest victim of this unfaithfulness is the steward himself. He closes the windows of heaven's blessing against himself.

For those who have never known the joy and satisfaction of giving proportionately to God, I highly recommend that you accept God's challenge and bring your tithes and offerings and experience new blessings from God.

For those who for years have experienced the blessings of rendering tithes, I would invite you to graduate from tithing and experience the added blessings of giving compassionately and sacrificially for the purposes of God — 15 percent, 20 percent, and more. In affluent times like these with the world battered, bleeding, hungry, and without Christ, can a devoted follower of Christ with genuine compassion in his heart feel comfortable giving a mere tithe?

As Christians we have experienced the abundant grace of God, the forgiveness of our sins, the indwelling Spirit of God, and other innumerable spiritual and material blessings. Each of us before God, with hearts of gratitude and compassion, must decide what giving in proportion to His gifts will mean. Warm, generous, cheerful, and grateful giving is more pleasing to Him than cold, calculating percentages and quotas.

For those who have enough for security, enough to meet foreseeable needs, why not join the royal ranks of persons like John Wesley, Adoniram Judson, William Colgate, A. A. Hyde, Charles Cowman, David Livingstone, and others, rendering all net income to the mighty purposes of God? No investment of possessions could result in greater good, yield richer dividends, or contribute more significantly to the glory of God, the welfare of mankind, and the joy of the giver. To become rich toward God by parting with earthly goods is a bargain par excellence.

It is encouraging to know that Americans gave around three billion dollars more in 1972 than the year before. Giving was up nine percent, and giving through wills was up 36 percent. However, we are still reminded that the average church member's giving falls shamefully below a half of the tithe. If we are truly interested in carrying out the Great Commission and in promoting the kingdom of God, we must take more seriously the challenge of Christian stewardship.

2

THE MEANING OF
CHRISTIAN STEWARDSHIP

After more than thirty years as a missionary to Africa, David Livingstone died on his knees. Friends removed his heart and buried it under an African tree. The body was dried in the sun, wrapped in cloth, tied to a pole, and carried hundreds of miles to the coast. From there it was shipped to England and buried in Westminster Abbey, almost a year after his death. David Livingstone's sense of stewardship is expressed in the following words:

> "I will place no value on anything I possess save in relation to the kingdom of God. If anything will advance the kingdom of God it shall be given away or kept, only as by the giving or the keeping of it I shall promote the glory of Him to whom I owe all my hopes in time and in eternity." [1]

His words as well as his life portray the attitude of a true steward of God. He placed his possessions under the lordship of Christ to be used for God's glory. He was conscious of the ownership of God and the stewardship of man.

The truth of the ownership of God and the stewardship of man is stamped indelibly on the pages of Scripture. Stewardship is a law of first magnitude in the economy of God, a primary principle in God's universe which if observed will bring great blessing and harmony. Man may violate it only at his own peril. Obedience to this law would have meant a paradise on this earth. Violation of the principle of stewardship has resulted in a world of violence, poverty, and suffering and a world of intolerable oppression.

Stewardship consists of a special relationship between man and his God. God richly bestows upon man personality, abilities, and possessions and holds him responsible for their use. He is to use them to promote God's interests in the world. These interests involve the best for man and for the universe. Only as God is recognized as sovereign and His will done are holiness and happiness of life possible for His creatures.

Stewardship is as much a part of theology as the atonement or the second coming of Christ, and the word "stewardship" best describes the true relationship between man and his God. The word implies trust, responsibility, partnership. A steward is entrusted with the possessions of another and manages them according to the will of the owner.

In Bible times a steward was the administrator of a family or estate. Often he was a slave. We see this relationship in the house of Abraham, with his trusted steward, who "ruled over all that Abraham had." Before Abraham had a son this steward was his heir. When Abraham wanted a wife for his son Isaac, he sent his trusted steward to pick a suitable bride. The steward was close to his master and was entrusted with the most important matters.

In Genesis 24 we see the position of trust and

19

authority held by Abraham's steward. "The servant took
ten camels of the camels of his master, and departed; for
all the goods of his master were in his hand" (v. 10).
"And the servant brought forth jewels of silver, and jewels
of gold, and raiment, and gave them to Rebekah: he gave
also to her brother and to her mother precious things"
(v. 53). He used his master's wealth and authority to
carry out his master's will.

In Egypt, Potiphar appointed Joseph steward over his
household. "And he made him overseer over his house,
and all that he had he put into his hand. . . . And he
left all that he had in Joseph's hand; and he knew not
ought he had, save the bread which he did eat" (Gen.
39:4, 6). Later when Joseph became ruler of Egypt he
had his own steward who "ruled his house." This steward
prepared entertainment for Joseph's brothers. He put the
money in the sack of each of the brothers and Joseph's
cup in Benjamin's sack. This steward arrested the brothers
and brought them back.

The word "stewardship" occurs infrequently in the Bible,
but the concept is present throughout the Old and New
Testaments. It may be helpful to notice a few definitions
given by various authors.

Definitions of Stewardship

"Stewardship is to the Christian what a mainspring is
to a watch. A watch cannot run without a mainspring. A
church cannot 'go,' however vigorously you shake it,
without a dynamic motive." [2]

"Stewardship is the management of life and all its
resources for God and for the good of all."

"Christian stewardship is a lifetime disposition of self,
and all that self includes, upon the flaming altar of
service. The ideal steward can withhold nothing, waste

nothing, dissipate nothing, clutch nothing to his breast." [3]

"Stewardship is partnership with Christ, through the Holy Spirit, in fulfilling the purposes of God in the world." [4]

"When Jesus becomes our Lord we become His stewards. There can be no lordship of Jesus without stewardship on the part of His followers. Lordship implies stewardship: one cannot exist without the other." [5]

"The miracle of stewardship, like the miracle of seed and harvest, is progressive. The more one gives, the more he receives. He doesn't always receive in kind, but what he receives is more generous and precious than what he gives, for God's gifts are always better than ours. This doesn't make good sense in ordinary logic, but it is the kind of sense God has written in the stewardship mystery. Every faithful steward has experienced the truth of it, and many publicly testified to its truthfulness." [6]

Many definitions are limited to the stewardship of material possessions. The ones given above include life and all the resources entrusted to the Christian by his Lord.

In this book Christian stewardship will mean *the receiving and sharing of God's bounteous gifts, managing them for the best promotion of God's purposes in the world.*

From the beginning God had a great and benevolent plan for His world. God created man to be His partner, His steward. God equipped His stewards with natural and spiritual resources to promote His cause. Faithfulness to his trust would mean sharing the joy, the power, the peace, and the glory of God, while unfaithfulness would result in futility, frustration, and defeat. Fulfilling his trust and doing the will of God today will always mean serving the best interests of one's fellowmen, resulting in God's

21

blessing on him. When man seeks selfish ends, he degrades himself, wrongs others and works against the benevolent purposes of God.

What These Definitions Imply

A sound theology of stewardship must include the following points. The faithful steward will always be aware of these.

1. God is Creator and Owner of all things. "The earth is the Lord's, and the fulness thereof" (Ps. 24:1). God permits man to inhabit the earth and to reap its fruits. He graciously bestows upon man the gifts of personality, abilities, time, and possessions. He gives man the ability to get wealth. All that we are and all that we have become a trust from God.

2. Man is a steward of God's creation and of God's gifts. God has given these gifts to man to manage according to the will of the Owner and for His glory. Man is to care for the earth, subdue it, and have dominion over it, but not to exploit it.

3. The Christian steward has a responsibility not only to God but also to his fellowmen. "None of us lives to himself." The Christian steward may not ask, "Am I my brother's keeper?" If he sees his brother in need and shuts his heart of compassion against him, how does the love of God dwell in him? As God has a deep love and concern for His people and the world, so must His stewards. To promote the purposes of God means to promote the welfare of people about us.

4. Good stewardship implies generous, proportionate giving. God as Owner graciously permits His people to reap the fruits of the earth and asks a portion of the increase. He does this for the promotion of His purposes and for the discipline of His stewards. From the beginning He asked

sacrifices, firstfruits and firstlings and tithes and offerings. The Christian steward regularly will "set aside as God prospers." As he freely receives he will freely give.

5. Christians are also stewards of the gospel, the manifold grace of God. We are the ministers of reconciliation. As we experience the goodness of God and appreciate His boundless blessings, and as we realize His love and concern for the lost world, we will say like the Apostle Paul, "Necessity is laid upon me; yea, woe is unto me, if I preach not the gospel" (1 Cor. 9:16). We will gladly use our talents, as well as possessions, for the furtherance of the gospel.

6. The Christian steward must give account of his stewardship to God. Daniel Webster was once asked what was the greatest thought that had ever entered his mind. His reply was, "My accountability to God." Good stewardship on the part of God would demand that He hold man accountable for the gifts that He entrusts to him. Man should be aware that he cannot squander, exploit, or use selfishly what God has entrusted to him for proper use without paying the penalty for unfaithfulness.

In stewardship the principle of rewards and penalties applies. Faithfulness brings the approval of God, the enlargement of our stewardship, and the sharing of the Lord's joy. Unfaithfulness brings the disapproval of God, diminished opportunities, and alienation from our Lord. Accountability of the steward is emphasized in many of the parables of Jesus and in many of His other teachings.

The Open Hand to Receive and the Active Hand to Give

Paul Tillich, the theologian, is credited with saying that religion is first, an open hand to receive a gift, and second, an active hand to distribute gifts; a good definition for stewardship. Contrary to what some people think, stewardship is not primarily giving, but rather receiving. Unless man receives, he has nothing to give. Paul tells the Corinthians that they are full and rich and reign as kings. But he asks them, "Didn't God give you everything you have?" (1 Cor. 4:7, TEV). Their hands had been open and received much. Paul now wants them to be active to give as stewards of God.

All man is and all he possesses have come from God. God's covenant with the patriarchs was, "I will bless you, and you shall be a blessing." Only as He blessed them could they be a blessing. Only as we open our hands to receive His gifts can we distribute gifts to others. Christian stewardship is first of all learning to receive.

We can be stewards of life only as we receive that life from God. We can be stewards of abilities and gifts only as the Spirit gives them to us. Paul tells us in 1 Corinthians 12 that there are diversities of gifts but they are all given by one Spirit. To one is given the gift of wisdom, to others the gifts of knowledge, faith, healing, working miracles, tongues, interpretation of tongues.

We cannot be stewards in witnessing unless we receive from God the power to witness (Acts 1:8). We can be stewards of the gospel only as we have received the gospel. Paul tells the Corinthians, "I received from the Lord what I also delivered to you" (11:23). He strongly insists when he writes the Galatians that the gospel he preached was not received from man but from God. Moses told Israel, "Give as you are able, according as the Lord has blessed you" (Deut. 16:17, *The Living Bible*).

Peter says, "As every man hath received the gift, even so minister the same one to another, as good stewards of the manifold grace of God" (1 Pet. 4:10). The Christian steward has an open hand to receive the gifts of God and a willing hand to share with others. When he is in a right relationship with God, then God can bless him and he in turn can be a blessing.

Conflicting Philosophies of Life

Few things determine more what a man will be than his philosophy of life. Many factors help him form his philosophy, and how he looks at life determines in a large way what his character will be, what decisions he will make, and whether he will be a blessing or a curse in the world — whether he will be a Judas or an Apostle Paul; an Al Capone or a D. L. Moody.

The philosophy of stewardship should become a dynamic force in the lives of Christians, motivating their decisions and their lives. Many worldly philosophies common today stand in direct conflict with the principle of stewardship. In his book, *The Horizons of Stewardship,* [7] H. C. Weber lists a number of these philosophies: (1) pigpen philosophy; (2) bingo philosophy; (3) main street philosophy; (4) pagan philosophy; (5) materialistic philosophy.

In pigpen philosophy the motive is indulgence, satisfying fleshly passions and lusts. As a farm boy I often witnessed the squealing and shoving of pigs as they tried to get their snouts in the trough and fill their bellies. They cared not what happened to the other pigs so long as they could satisfy their own appetites. Paul speaks of people with this philosophy, "whose god is their belly." They think only of satisfying their own desires; the needs, the feelings, and the welfare of others do not concern them.

This philosophy motivates people to traffic in alcohol, drugs, prostitution, and other forms of evil that degrade, demoralize, and damn the bodies and souls of millions.

These people will attempt to influence civic groups, police departments, and courts and legislatures to legalize, permit, and condone social evils. If they can satisfy their greed for gain and selfish interests, they are ready to sacrifice the welfare of other individuals, of society, and of the nation. They are parasites of society.

The bingo philosophy with its slogan "something for nothing" has tremendous appeal in today's society. One can hardly get a seed catalog without being offered a "chance" at a large sum of money. "Trash mail" these days contains application blanks to appeal to whatever bingo philosophy may be sticking in us. Many blanks are filled and sent in, for "we might be lucky for once." Persons with this philosophy often take the attitude that society or the government owes them a living. They are quick to climb any "share-the-wealth" bandwagon. This philosophy can rob people of their self-respect and of their ambition to make good. It can lead people to forsake thrift, labor, and honest ways of making a living.

Many state legislatures apply pressure to legalize lotteries and other types of gambling. Others are urging that racetrack gambling be permitted. Some urge that churches be permitted to play bingo. Churches with this philosophy try to find painless ways of supporting the church and missions, appealing to the gambling spirit, with raffles, bingo, and lotteries. This method of securing funds for the Lord's work does not represent Christian stewardship.

Main street philosophy, rather common today, takes on a respectable appearance. It emphasizes thrift and frugality, but often assumes proportions of possessiveness and covetousness. The desire to possess is normal and good when rightly used, but when it turns into covetousness and greed it can corrupt and destroy. This philosophy

26

is something of a combination of the other worldly philosophies. It justifies keeping up with the Joneses, feathering our own bed, and bathing in luxury, regardless of the suffering and needs of the world about us.

Pagan philosophy centers everything around self. Self is at the center, and God is on the periphery, if considered at all. It says, "All that I can get my hands on is mine to use as I please; the world is mine to exploit." This philosophy spawns cynicism, suspicion, pride, and arrogance. The following jingle expresses it well:

I gave a little party this afternoon at three.
'Twas very small,
Three guests in all —
Just I, myself, and me.
Myself ate up the sandwiches,
While I drank up the tea,
And it was I
Who ate the pie
And passed the cake to me.
— Author unknown

The philosophy of materialism is the chief foe to Christian principles and attitudes. Success and wealth are measured by one's material possessions. What a man has, becomes more important than what he is. This philosophy is one of today's gods. We need to hear Jesus again as He says, "A man's life consisteth not in the abundance of the things which he possesseth." This philosophy helps many men become millionaires, but it keeps churches poor, permits millions of people to live in poverty, and makes world evangelism impossible. The rich fool, a good example of this way, met a tragic end which may well be the lot of many who follow his example. "But they that will be rich fall into temptation and a snare, and into many foolish and hurtful lusts, which drown men in

27

destruction and perdition" (1 Tim. 6:9). "Ye cannot serve God and mammon."

The philosophy of Christian stewardship stands in sharp contrast to the above philosophies. It is concerned also about things, but does not place them at the center of life as the other philosophies do. Christian stewardship places God at the center and things on the periphery. It rejects self-indulgence, selfishness, and things as primary motivating principles, and puts in their place partnership with God. Of all the philosophies, only Christian steward-ship puts things in the right perspective. God is sovereign. People are of more value than things. Money, instead of serving selfish ends, becomes a tool in the steward's hands for the promotion of the kingdom of God and for the welfare of fellowmen. Wealth is not an end in itself or a means of satisfying selfish interests, but a useful means toward worthy ends. Instead of loving things and using people, the Christian loves people and uses things.

Our Definition of Stewardship

Stewardship is receiving and sharing God's bounteous gifts and managing them for the best promotion of God's purposes in the world.

God's gifts are the resources He entrusts to man with which to promote His kingdom. God gives man life, body, mind, abilities, time, and possessions. He has given us His Word, redemption, and the Holy Spirit. He holds man accountable for the proper use of these gifts. They were given, not to be used for selfish purposes, but to promote His purposes which embrace the best welfare of man and God's creation. Therefore we need to have a right concept of God, of the purposes of God, and of man himself.

3

THE GOD
OF THE STEWARD

Adam and Eve doubted God's word because they thought He was withholding something good from them. Thus they disobeyed Him and ate of the forbidden fruit. The servant in the parable of the talents saw his lord as a "hard master" and hid his talent in the earth. The servants who believed that their lord was delaying His coming were unfaithful in their stewardship. All these had inadequate concepts of their lord and failed to be good stewards. We cannot be good stewards if we have vague or wrong concepts of God.

To accept the "God is dead" concept would deal a deathblow to Christian stewardship. To embrace the deist concept of God, that He is no longer active or present in the universe, would also make true stewardship meaningless. To accept the pantheistic view of God, as many youth are doing today, would shatter the philosophy of stewardship of the gospel. Dynamic Christian stewardship will never be possible when men do not believe in the love, holiness, and justice of God as portrayed in the Bible.

A true understanding of God will result in grateful and joyous stewardship. A major factor, therefore, in determining the stewardship of man is a correct under-standing of God and a right relationship to Him. Only a true and high view of God and His Word can assure faithful stewardship. When God becomes real to man, he will want to faithfully do His will. We see this in the lives of many Bible characters who had a vision of God which affected their attitudes and changed their lives.

David Senses the Greatness of God

When King David realized the greatness, the glory, and the goodness of God, he exclaimed, "Thine, O Lord, is the greatness, and the power, and the glory, and the victory, and the majesty: for all that is in the heaven and in the earth is thine: thine is the kingdom, O Lord, and thou art exalted as head above all. . . . And in thine hand is power and might; and in thine hand it is to make great, and to give strength" (1 Chron. 29:11, 12).

This high and holy concept of God caused David to want to build Him a dwelling place. This understanding of God led him to willingly consecrate thousands of talents of gold and silver, and wood, iron, marble, and precious stones in abundance. His faith in the Divine inspired him to sing out, "Great is the Lord, and greatly to be praised; and his greatness is unsearchable. . . . I will speak of the glorious honour of thy majesty, and of thy wondrous works" (Ps. 145:3, 5).

Psalm 103 reveals vividly David's sense of the good-ness and mercy of God. David sees God as the One who forgives sins, heals diseases, delivers from destruction, crowns with loving-kindness and tender mercies. He sees One whose mercy is from everlasting to everlasting and One who is long-suffering and plenteous in mercy. Time and again David experienced these things in his life. Six different times in the Psalm he cries out, "Bless the Lord."

David's lofty concept of God and His relationship to His people caused the praises of God to flow from his pen and from his lips. It gave him a love for God and for the commandments of God, "Oh, how I love thy law." It gave him a driving desire to fellowship with God. "One thing have I desired of the Lord, that will I seek after; that I may dwell in the house of the Lord all the days of my life, to behold the beauty of the Lord, and to enquire in his temple" (Ps. 27:4).

As a proper concept of God led David to do God's will, so it will inspire in us a desire to be His faithful stewards. The opposite is also true. If we have an inadequate concept of God, we will be sure to fail in our commitment to Him and in rendering to Him what is His.

Isaiah Sees the Lord

Isaiah caught a glimpse of the Lord and heard the seraphim crying, "Holy, holy, holy, is the Lord of hosts: the whole earth is full of his glory" (Is. 6). In this glimpse of the holy God Isaiah saw his own unworthiness as he said, "Woe is me! . . . I am a man of unclean lips . . . for mine eyes have seen the King, the Lord of hosts." In ready response to the question of who will go he answers, "Here am I; send me." When God becomes real, His people will freely offer themselves and their possessions. Stinginess in giving is the result of an inadequate sense of God and an improper relationship with Him.

Moses Meets God

Few men have seen God and experienced His presence as did Moses. He met God at the burning bush, took his shoes off his feet, and hid his face (Ex. 2:5, 6). On Mt. Sinai he spent days in God's presence. After Israel's safe passage through the Red Sea, Moses led the children of

Israel in singing, "I will sing unto the Lord, for he hath triumphed gloriously. . . . The Lord is my strength and song, and he is become my salvation: he is my God, and I will prepare him an habitation; my father's God, and I will exalt him. . . . Who is like unto thee, O Lord, among the gods? Who is like thee, glorious in holiness, fearful in praises, doing wonders?" (Ex. 15).

This high and exalted sense of greatness and goodness of God inspired Moses to make a total commitment to God and to give himself a living sacrifice for the promotion of God's cause and for the blessing of God's people. He was willing even to have his own name blotted out for Israel's good and God's glory. Moses exemplifies supreme stewardship, the result of a high and holy concept of God and a love for His people.

Jacob's Ladder

In a dream Jacob saw a ladder reaching to heaven with angels ascending and descending. At the top stood the Lord, who promised to bless and prosper him and bring him to his home again. Jacob worshiped Him and said, "Surely the Lord is in this place. . . . This is none other but the house of God, and this is the gate of heaven." Early in the morning he arose, set up a stone, and poured oil on it. In gratitude he made a solemn vow. Because he had seen the Lord and heard the Lord's promise of blessing, he promised to give a tenth of all the Lord would give him (Gen. 28:10-22). Genuine gratitude to God for His promises and blessings will result in generous giving, while ingratitude clogs the springs of giving.

◦ ◦ ◦

Persons, talents, and possessions to promote the gospel and the church of Christ on earth will be available when people truly meet God and experience His Spirit in their lives. When Saul of Tarsus saw the Lord and heard Him speak, he asked, "Lord, what wilt thou have me to do?" He was ready to leave position, home, and possessions, and give all for Christ. He was ready to suffer persecutions, floggings, imprisonment, shipwreck, and martyrdom that the cause of Christ might go forward.

When the disciples had witnessed the crucifixion, the resurrection, and the ascension of the Lord and had been filled with the Holy Spirit, they were willing to go everywhere preaching the Word. They were willing to part with possessions that others might have food and clothing. Thousands of persons since then have met the Lord and have forsaken homes, loved ones, and possessions and have followed where God led. Others have met the Lord but were not asked to leave home and possessions. They are also God's faithful stewards in their home communities, dedicating their time, talents, and possessions for the furtherance of the gospel.

God as Steward

God has set an example of stewardship for His people. He voluntarily elected to commit His attributes and powers to the law of stewardship. Ralph Spalding Cushing, a prominent promoter of stewardship the first half of this century, said that perhaps the most impressive fact in the whole universe is that God is not only sovereign Lord to whom we must all give account but that He set a high and holy example of voluntarily placing Himself under the law of stewardship.

The example of such consecration of the total resources of God is staggering. "Behind the laws of stewardship which pervade the universe is love — love divine. . . . It is a great moment in any life when one makes the discovery that law and love are inseparable, because both spring from the heart and character of God." [1] Cushman suggests that "the Spirit brooding on the waters" indicates God's restlessness until all His vast resources are placed at the disposal of others. It would be contrary to the character of God, as to any good steward, to lavish upon Himself His powers and resources.

God's Stewardship Power

The Scriptures tell us of the might and the power of God. As a good steward He could not lavish this power on Himself nor let it lie idle. He used His mighty powers to create the heavens and the earth. How His majestic power is shown in His creation! "The heavens declare the glory of God; and the firmament sheweth his handywork."

The vastness, the magnitude, and the splendor of His creation transcend man's comprehension. "Astronomers tell us that the Milky Way, the galaxy to which our earth and solar system belong, consists of over 30,000,000,000 suns, many of them immensely larger than our sun, which is a million and a half times larger than the earth. The Milky Way is shaped like a thin watch, its diameter from rim to rim being 200,000 light years. A light year is the distance that travels in a year at the rate of 186,000 miles a second. And there are at least 100,000 galaxies like the Milky Way, some of them millions of light years apart. And all this may be but a tiny speck in what is beyond in the infinite, endless stretch of space." [2]

Some later scientists say there are more than 100 billion galaxies with tens of billions of stars and suns in each! God told Abraham that his seed would be as numerous as the stars of heaven and as the sand of the sea. I used to think that here was a discrepancy, a handful of sand would equal the stars. But one astronomer has said that the stars of heaven may be as many as the grains of sand on our· seashores.

We are overwhelmed when we think of the reaches of space. If in the eleventh century BC they would have had airplanes, and if in the year 1117 BC, during the days of Samson, a plane would have left the earth with the planet Neptune as the destination and would have traveled night and day at 100 miles per hour it would reach its destination some time this year, AD 1973.

But Neptune is relatively near the earth, less than 3 billion miles. It would take light a little less than five hours to reach from Neptune to the earth. Astronomers tell us there is a star that may be seen today that is so far from the earth that it took its light 1,500,000 years to reach the earth, traveling nearly 6 million million miles per year. [3] With the psalmist we cry out, "O Lord, how manifold are thy works! in wisdom hast thou made them all: the earth is full of thy riches" (Ps. 104:24).

God's Stewardship of Love

"God is love." As a good steward of that love God could not simply bestow it upon Himself. He created celestial beings, and terrestrial beings whom He called His sons and with whom He could share His love, glory, and power and with whom He could fellowship. He created the hosts of heaven, an innumerable company of angels (Heb. 12:22; Rev. 5:11). These were to be His ministering spirits, standing in His presence, worshiping, praising, and adoring Him, carrying out His will. [4] They share His joy and His glory and rejoice in His works (Job 38:7; Lk. 15:10).

Not only are the angels God's stewards in promoting His will in heaven, but they also are assigned duties on earth among men. [5] The angels will be the reapers and attend Christ at His coming. [6] They will pour out the vials of God's wrath upon the earth (Rev. 16) and bind

Satan and cast him into the bottomless pit (Rev. 20:1, 2).

Had it not been for the sin and disobedience of man, no doubt there would have been joyous and meaningful cooperation between God's celestial and terrestrial beings, as together they promoted the purposes of God in His kingdom. When the kingdom of God has fully come, redeemed man and the angels in His presence will share His praises, His joy, and His glory. [7]

Seemingly, in the beginning, both in heaven and on earth God's complete will was being done. Joy, peace, and harmony prevailed. "The morning stars sang together, and all the sons of God shouted for joy" (Job 38:7). His rule on earth and in heaven was universal and unchallenged until in heaven Lucifer set his will against the will of God (Is. 14:12-14), and man went against God's will on earth.

As a result of this rebellion and disobedience there are two kingdoms — the kingdom of light and the kingdom of darkness. Satan is now vying with God for the minds and souls of men. But God continued to be a good steward of His love, sharing and giving freely. He gave His Son to atone for man's sin and to bring him back into right relationship with Himself. God came to earth in Christ, reconciling the world to Himself. "Behold, what manner of love!" Love so abounding should challenge us to a grateful response and dedication of ourselves to the stewardship of the gospel.

God Is Sovereign Owner

Fundamental to a proper concept of God is to recognize Him as the Owner of all, by right of creation and by right of redemption. Too many people are guilty of the same error as was the rich fool in the parable of Jesus: "my goods," "my barns," "my soul." The idea that man is owner is pagan and false. Man is only the steward of God's world and its resources.

But many people are spiritually and socially immature. Like the infant, anything they can grasp is "mine." If I am strong enough or clever enough to take it from others, it is "mine." We need to grow in grace and knowledge, and realize that God is Owner. What we have is only a trust to share and administer for His glory. The Scriptures strongly declare that God is Owner:

Genesis 14:18-22. Both Melchizedek and Abraham recognized God as possessor of heaven and earth.

Exodus 19:5. "For all the earth is mine."

Leviticus 25:23. "The land shall not be sold for ever: for the land is mine."

1 Chronicles 29:11. Here David acknowledges God's ownership. "For all that is in heaven and in the earth is thine: thine is the kingdom, O Lord, and thou art exalted as head above all."

Psalm 24:1. "The earth is the Lord's, and the fulness thereof; the world, and they that dwell therein."

Psalm 50:10. "For every beast of the forest is mine, and the cattle upon a thousand hills."

Haggai 2:8. "The silver is mine, and the gold is mine, saith the Lord of hosts."

The Apostle Paul declares that even our spirits and bodies belong to God. To recognize and acknowledge the ownership of God is a fundamental principle of Christian stewardship. If we fail in this acknowledgment, we will fail in stewardship.

The Holiness of God

> "Who else is like the Lord among the gods?
> Who is glorious in holiness like Him?
> Who is so awesome in splendor,
> A wonder-working God?" (Ex. 15:11, *The Living Bible*).

The steward must see God as a holy God, totally separate from sin. Sin defiles, debases, enslaves, and destroys, and is totally contrary and inimical to the purposes of God. The nature of God makes it impossible for Him to tolerate evil in Himself, in His stewards, or in His world. At the culmination of His kingdom all that defiles and is unholy will be done away, out of His presence. He says to His stewards, "Be ye holy; for I am holy." The steward must cultivate holiness of life and promote holiness in the earth. Without holiness no man can see the Lord.

The Justice of God

> "For all of us must appear before the judgment seat of Christ, so that each one may receive what he deserves, according to what he has done, good or bad, in his bodily life" (2 Cor. 5:10, TEV).

A proper concept of God must include a sense of His justice. The holiness and righteousness of God demand perfect justice on His part. Sin must be punished and righteousness rewarded. The accountability of the steward of God is emphasized many times in the Scriptures, both by precept and example. This causes no undue concern on the part of the faithful steward, but should cause the unfaithful steward to consider his ways.

Many striking examples of God's justice occur throughout the Bible as He dealt with His people. We find two of these in Genesis 3 and 4.

In the third chapter God calls Adam and Eve to

account for violating the principle of divine ownership. He had entrusted them with the trees of the garden but had specifically reserved one tree. He wanted to remind them that He was Owner and that they were stewards. When they failed to recognize God's sovereign ownership and used for selfish purposes what God had reserved for Himself, God drove them from the garden. The justice meted out for disregarding God's property rights and for disobedience was severe. When God drove Adam from the garden, He was not merely punishing a naughty boy. He was firing an unfaithful steward. If Adam could not be trusted with the forbidden fruit, could he now be trusted with the tree of life?

> "Because you listened to your wife and ate the fruit when I told you not to, I have placed a curse upon the soil. All your life you will struggle to extract a living from it. It will grow thorns and thistles for you, and you shall eat its grasses. All your life you will sweat to master it, until your dying day" (Gen. 3:17-19, *The Living Bible*).

In Genesis 4 we have another case of God meting out justice for disobedience. Here God refuses to accept an offering, "offered aright, but not divided aright," according to the Septuagint. The severity of the penalty would indicate that Cain must have been well aware of what his sin was. A number of the church fathers believed that Cain offered rightly but did not offer proportionately. Josephus says, "Cain was not only very wicked in other respects, but he was wholly intent on getting." The Council of Seville passed a canon that read, "If anyone does not tithe everything . . . let the curse of God which He inflicted on Cain for not rightly tithing be heaped on him."

Whatever the exact violation may have been, we see that God's greatest concern was for His people. In the first case God asks, "Adam, where are you?" In the fourth chapter the question is, "Where is Abel thy brother?" His first concern was not, "Where is my fruit?" or "Where is my portion of the fruit of the ground?" The major concern in the mind of God was, "What happened to Adam and Eve?" and "What happened to Cain and Abel?"

It is tragic when the work of missions must be curtailed for lack of funds. It is unfortunate when people must be naked and hungry because of man's selfishness. But the greatest tragedy is what happens to God's people who violate stewardship principles and permit such conditions to exist and who misappropriate for selfish purposes what God wants reserved for Him.

Let us briefly notice a few other examples of the justice of God and accountability of man. In Leviticus 10, Nadab and Abihu offered strange fire before the Lord "which he commanded them not. And there went out fire from the Lord, and devoured them."

In Numbers 12 Aaron and Miriam defied the authority of Moses. "And the anger of the Lord was kindled against them . . . and, behold, Miriam became leprous, white as snow" (vv. 9, 10).

Another striking example of the justice of God and the accountability of man is found in Joshua 7. Before Israel crossed the Jordan, God instructed them about the procedure for taking the city. He said, "The city shall be devoted [marginal reading], even it and all that are therein, to the Lord. . . . And ye, in any wise keep yourselves from the devoted thing, lest ye make yourselves accursed, when ye take of the devoted thing, and make the camp of Israel a curse, and trouble it" (Josh. 6:17, 18).

The word that is translated "accursed" in the King James is the same word that is translated at other places "devoted." The first city that God was going to deliver to

Israel was to be "devoted," dedicated to God. "But all the silver, and gold, and vessels of brass and iron, are consecrated unto the Lord: they shall come into the treasury of the Lord" (6:19). As God reserved one tree in the garden, as He reserved the first year's fruit, and as He reserved the firstborn, so He reserved the first city as a token, as a reminder, of His divine ownership of the land. Later Israel could take the spoils.

"But there was sin among the Israelites. God's command to destroy everything except that which was reserved for the Lord's treasury was disobeyed. Achan took some loot for himself, and the Lord was very angry with the entire nation of Israel because of this" (Josh. 7:1, *The Living Bible*). Covetousness, the love of money, caused Achan to disobey the commandment of the Lord. Achan is called to account and he and his family were destroyed. Also, because of the sin of this one man Israel was soundly defeated at Ai.

God strictly held Israel accountable in His dealings with them. In Exodus 13 God gave Moses various instructions. In verse 12 He referred to the firstlings of cattle as belonging to Him. In the next verse He says, "A firstborn donkey may be purchased back from the Lord in exchange for a lamb or baby goat; but if you decide not to trade, the donkey shall be killed" (*The Living Bible*).

A second example is found in Numbers 3. Here God takes the children of Levi in exchange for the firstborn. He tells Moses to number the males of the tribe of Levi, and the firstborn males. The count revealed 22,000 Levites and 22,273 firstborn. God asked Israel to pay five shekels to Aaron and the priests for each of the 273, the number of firstborn in excess of the Levites. God wants His people to be responsible people. He is gracious and fair in His dealings with us, and in turn, expects us to be fair with

Him. "It is required in stewards, that a man be found faithful."

Many parables of Jesus teach us the justice of God and the accountability of the steward. They always teach rewards for faithful stewardship but penalties for unfaithfulness.

God's Character Seen in What He Hates and Loves

The steward of God will try to avoid what God hates and to embrace what He loves. He will "abhor that which is evil; cleave to that which is good."

God loves righteousness, but hates wickedness and iniquity. (Heb. 1:9; Ps. 45:7.)

God loves obedience and hates disobedience. (1 Sam. 15:21, 22.)

God loves faith and hates unbelief. (Jn. 3:36.)

God loves the peacemaker, but hates those who love violence. (Mt. 5:9; Ps. 11:5.)

God loves humility but hates pride. (Prov. 23:12.)

God loves a cheerful giver, but hates covetousness. (2 Cor. 9:7; Col. 3:5.)

"Six things the Lord hates,
seven things are detestable to him:
a proud eye, a false tongue,
hands that shed innocent blood,
a heart that forges thoughts of mischief,
and feet that run swiftly to do evil,
a false witness telling a pack of lies,
and one who stirs up quarrels between brothers" (Prov. 6:16-19, NEB).

We are stewards of a marvelous God: perfect in holiness, justice, love, and mercy, and infinite in power. He wants to share with His stewards His peace, love, and power. He bountifully bestows upon us rich gifts of personality, abilities, and possessions to be used for God's glory. He holds man accountable for the proper use of these gifts, liberally rewarding the faithful steward, but punishing unfaithfulness.

4

THE ETERNAL
PURPOSES OF GOD

"I have spoken it, I will also bring it to pass;
I have purposed it, I will also do it" (Is. 46:11).

The Christian steward receives generous physical and
spiritual resources from the Creator and Redeemer. He
dedicates these willingly to the promotion of God's purposes in the earth. The purposes of God are eternal —
the same yesterday, today, and forever. In the first chapters of Ephesians the Apostle Paul tells us of God's
eternal purposes in the past, present, and future.

In the eternity past we were chosen by the Father
to be holy and blameless, destined to be sons of God in
Jesus Christ, "for the praise of his glorious grace." Before the worlds were framed God planned for man's redemption and glorification.

In the present we stand redeemed by the Son, our
transgressions forgiven. The mystery of His will has been
revealed to us — the uniting of all things in heaven and
on earth in Christ, and "to the praise of his glory."

In the future, having been sealed by the Holy Spirit,
our promised heritage, our full redemption, is guaranteed,
and again "for the praise of his glory."

Thus, the purpose of creation, of redemption, and of man's sanctification and glorification is for the praise of God's glory. At the same time this purpose results in the glory, the joy, and the welfare of God's creation. What enhances God's glory enhances the glory of His creation. What dishonors God harms His creation. The eternal purpose of God in creating and redeeming the world was that creation might share and portray His glory, majesty, and righteousness.

Paul expresses and exemplifies this purpose, the praise of God's glory, in the opening verses of Ephesians, "Blessed be the God and Father of our Lord Jesus Christ, who has blessed us in Christ with every spiritual blessing in the heavenly places." This was the song of the universe before the worlds were formed, when the stars sang together and the sons of God shouted for joy (Job 38:7). All nature praises God: the butterflies by their beauty and grace, the birds by their song and flight, the flowers by their color and fragrance, the frogs and crickets by their croaking and chirping. "Bless the Lord, all his works in all places of his dominion; bless the Lord, O my soul."

"Blessed be God" is the perpetual strain of the Old Testament from Abraham to the prophets, from Moses at the Red Sea to Daniel in the lions' den.

"Blessing, and glory, and wisdom, and thanksgiving, and honour, and power, and might, be unto our God for ever and ever" will be the praises of the combined choir of the redeemed and the angels in the heavenly kingdom (Rev. 7:12).

Man's Place in God's Creation

God created the earth to be the habitation of man (Is. 45:18). He created man to be His habitation, the

45

temple of His Spirit. Man was made in God's image — in knowledge, righteousness, and true holiness: [1] just a little lower than Himself and crowned with glory and honor (Ps. 8:5). This purpose of God for man becomes evident when we see God's purpose for redeemed man. God wants man totally restored to His image. In this restoration man becomes the abiding place of God (Eph. 2:22), the temple of God.

John emphasizes this in 1 John 4:12-15 (TEV), "If we love one another God lives in us. . . . This is how we are sure that we live in God and he lives in us: he has given us his Spirit. . . . Whoever declares that Jesus is the Son of God, God lives in him." If this is God's will for redeemed man, it must have been His will before the Fall.

In the Old Testament God expresses His desire to live among His people. Through sin man lost the image of God and therefore could not be God's temple. Since God could not live in unredeemed man He chose to live among them, to dwell in the tabernacle and the temple.

What a great purpose God had for man! What love, what joy, what peace and power were to be man's! For the God of love, joy, peace, and power would be dwelling in him. The evils that now plague man's society — selfishness, poverty, hate, war, injustice, crime, disease, and death are totally contrary to God's plan for His community of people.

When man listened to the voice of the serpent and ate of the forbidden tree the temple of God was defiled. Man became possessed with the spirit of evil and self-love instead of the Spirit of God and self-giving. But in the eternal purposes of God He had determined, before the worlds were formed, to have a redeemed people and a redeemed church of Christ. For the praise of His glory

God prepared for a redeemed society on earth. Furthermore, before the foundation of the world He had prepared a heavenly kingdom which His people shall yet inherit (Mt. 25:34). The Lamb had been slain before the foundation of the world (Rev. 25:34).

After man sinned the Creator became the Redeemer. The Spirit of God who had been evicted from His temple began to strive with men (Gen. 6:3). Men of faith found grace in the eyes of God (Gen. 6:9), and God made His covenant with them. Their faith was imputed to them for righteousness. God's great purpose for the reconciliation of the world was now in motion. Men of God justified by faith became stewards of God in preparing the way of the Lord.

God's Cosmic Plan

The Bible tells us how God is preparing a people for Himself. Perhaps the most fitting designation for His people would be "stewards of God." The people of God are the stewards of God. The Apostle Paul wanted the Corinthians to regard him as a servant of Christ and a steward of the mysteries of God. What could be more thrilling and challenging than to be a steward of God!

Jesus was the "express image" of the Father (Heb. 1:3). As a steward He perfectly performed the will of God. Today a steward is one who does the will of the Father. The will of God, the purposes of God, include the highest good for man and for the world. Being stewards of God means that we are engaged in the noblest, the best, the most glorious, and most rewarding endeavors possible. What great things God had in store for His people! But as Paul tells us in Romans 3:23, *The Living Bible*, "Yes, all have sinned; all fall short of God's glorious ideal."

The high privilege of being people of God and all that

is involved in this relationship are beyond human comprehension. "Eye hath not seen, nor ear heard, neither have entered into the heart of man, the things which God hath prepared for them that love him" (1 Cor. 2:9).

In the October 27, 1972, issue of *Christianity Today* Howard A. Snyder writes, "One perspective for viewing God's cosmic plan is to see it as the calling and preparation of a people (Gen. 1:28). God's promise to Abraham was, 'I will make you a great nation' (Gen. 12:2), and He did. God chose the children of Israel, redeeming them from Egypt, saying, 'I will make you my people, and I will be your God' (Deut. 7:6). This theme echoes constantly through the Old Testament."

John Howard Yoder states, "The work of God is the calling of a people, whether in the Old Covenant or in the New." [2] The same idea is stressed by the late Harold S. Bender in his book, *These Are My People*. Note also John W. Miller's comment, "The goal of 'cosmic intelligence' is the peopling of the universe with mature personalities" (*Gospel Herald*, Jan. 17, 1973).

More than a hundred times in the Bible God speaks of "My people." Nearly as many times the writers of Scripture refer to "His people," meaning God's people. Numerous times God speaks of being their God, and they being His people. He molded them into a people in the furnace of Egypt. [3] He saw the affliction of His people (Ex. 3:7), and through Moses said to Pharaoh, "Let my people go." [4]

The Conflict of the Ages

The Bible is not only a story of God preparing a people; it is also the story of "The Conflict of the Ages," the conflict between good and evil, between God and Satan. It is the story of man's failure and his tendency to resist and reject the love of God. In his unbelief, arrogance, and pride man set his will against the will of God. Instead of promoting the will and the holy purposes of God, he has set himself up as god. He has worked against his own welfare and against the highest good for the world.

But the Bible is also the story of God persevering in His purposes, not permitting Satan or man to thwart His plans. He will have a people for Himself — a community of love, peace, and righteousness as He purposed in the beginning. Lenski in commenting on Romans 8:20, 21 says, "The original intent of God when He created a perfect creature world for perfect man shall be carried out in spite of man's Fall."

When the children of Adam became wicked, God made His covenant with Noah and his seed. When they rebelled against God, He chose Abraham and his children. They were to be His stewards. He formed them into a mighty nation, the people of God. Later because of unbelief and disobedience, God had to reject Israel. However, He did not despair in His purpose to have a people on the earth. He did not abandon man.

Man's Tragic Failure

God's plan for a community of love and righteousness received a setback when man failed the test of stewardship and took the forbidden fruit. It meant not only the fall of man but of God's creation as well. The effect of Adam's sin was cosmic. The serpent was cursed above all cattle and above every beast of the field. The ground was cursed for man's sake. Not only was man estranged from God but also the earth that was under the dominion of man. Man did not only cease to serve God's purposes but creation became "subject to futility" (Rom. 8:20, RSV), no longer serving the purposes God intended.

49

The great purpose of God after the Fall was to prepare a people, but now the major purpose was to redeem man and to reconcile the lost world to Himself. God's people now became also stewards of redemption, "preparing the way of the Lord." The patriarchs, Moses, Joshua, the judges, and the prophets, were the stewards of God, working with God in preparing His people Israel for the place they were to fill in His eternal purposes. Through them came the adoption, the covenants, the promises, and eventually the Savior.

The Scriptures tell us of God continually instructing, warning, chiding, disciplining, and pleading with His people to shape them into a community of faith and righteousness. In spite of all man's failures God will not be thwarted. The prophets and the Book of Revelation foretell the fulfillment of His purposes, the consummation of a community of righteousness, with His faithful stewards sharing His joy and His glory. He loves His people whom He has redeemed with an everlasting love and will present them to Himself without blemish.

God's purpose from the beginning was to form for Himself a community of righteousness, joy, and love. That community was realized in a limited way in His people Israel. It is being realized today in an imperfect way in His new Israel, the church. But in the ages to come He will have that perfect community of love with no injustice, unrighteousness, poverty, pain, sickness, or death.

God has been moving in history since the fall of man toward the culmination of His purposes. Men of faith have been His stewards in promoting these purposes. God's people today should willingly dedicate themselves, their talents, and possessions to God's purposes. Investing our resources in God's eternal community of righteousness will return rich dividends. It will mean eternal treasure laid up in God's kingdom. To the praise of His glorious grace God's stewards promote the advancement of His kingdom.

We should remember, however, that God is interested not only in man's reconciliation, He wants also to reconcile creation. As the Fall had cosmic effects, so there are cosmic purposes in redemption.

God Reconciling the World

Paul tells us in 2 Corinthians, "God was in Christ reconciling the world to himself" (5:19). We may be inclined to limit this to reconciling men and women to God. This of course is primary, but it was the "cosmos," His creation, He was reconciling.

The New International Commentary of the New Testament in commenting on this passage states, "The reconciliation is cosmic in effect. Applied in the first place to mankind; but since man, as crown of God's creation, in his Fall brought a curse upon the subordinate realm also, so in man's restoration the whole created order [cosmos] will be restored also. What the first Adam dragged down the second Adam raises up." In reconciliation, as in creation, the work of Christ has cosmic significance. [5]

Romans 8:18-25 is also pertinent to this concept of God's creation. Lenski in commenting on this passage in Romans paraphrases verses 18, 19, "Don't occupy your minds with your own trifling suffering. Think of the vast creature world groaning, and we with it, but having all its hope centered in us as sons of God, centered on us and on our deliverance." He suggests that this is mightier than Christian deliverance only, and that both the suffering and the glory in verse 18 involve the whole creature world. "The creature waits for the revelation of the sons of God" (verse 19).

Lenski further suggests that in Romans 8 the great fact that appears already in Genesis 1 and runs throughout all of Scripture, and is prominent in Revelation 21:1, comes fully to view: the unity of God's creation, Christ the head of all things in heaven and on earth (Eph. 1:10). Romans 8:20 tells us that the creature was made subject to vanity, or vainness. Because of the fall of man and the curse, the creature no longer serves the purposes God intended. Man abuses God's creation at every turn, and it in turn harms and destroys man. God did not intend it to be this way. The creature is subject to vainness, but not by its own will. But the creature waits for restoration, a hope given by God. Man's restoration will be through pure grace, for man willingly disobeyed. The restoration of the creature world will be simple justice.

Let us notice the reading of this passage from Romans as paraphrased in *The Living Bible:*

> "For all creation is waiting patiently and hopefully for that future day when God will resurrect his children. For on that day thorns and thistles, sin, death and decay — the things that overcame the world against its will at God's command — will all disappear, and the world around us will share in the glorious freedom from sin which God's children enjoy. For we know that even the things of nature, like animals and plants, suffer in sickness and death as they await this great event" (8:19-22).

Our Ministry of Reconciliation

A most important part of the stewardship of the Christian, a way in which he significantly contributes to the "praise of God's glory," is the ministry of reconciliation. "He has reconciled us men to himself through Christ, and he has enlisted us in this service of reconciliation" (2 Cor. 5:18, NEB). A good steward of God will earnestly engage himself and his resources in reconciling the world to God helping men become restored to God's image and helping His creation to conform to His purposes.

This most certainly means leading men and women to a saving faith in Jesus Christ. But it means more than this. Peter says we are stewards of the manifold grace of God. We are to be sure to use the gifts God has given us in helping each other, "passing on to others God's many kinds of blessings" (1 Pet. 4:10, *The Living Bible*). God's purpose is not only that men escape perdition but also that they be completely restored to His image.

The Ministry of Perfecting the Saints

Those who receive Christ become the children of God (John 1:12) and are baptized by the Spirit into the body of Christ (1 Cor. 12:13). There is now no condemnation to them that are in Christ; they have been redeemed from the curse of the law and have eternal life. However, man's full redemption and the redemption of God's creation are far from complete. Both the Scriptures and our own experience make that abundantly clear. We groan within ourselves, waiting for the "adoption as sons, the redemption of our bodies" (Rom. 8:23), and all creation groans and waits with us.

In Christ we are a new creation. As stated in Ephesians 4 we are given apostles, prophets, evangelists, pastors, and teachers "for the perfecting of the saints." We still must be brought into the unity of the faith, unto a perfect man, unto the measure of the stature of the fullness of Christ. Even though we have been raised with Christ in newness of life, we must mortify the deeds of the body. Many things must be put off and many more put on (Col. 3:5-18).

As Christians we glory in the cross and resurrection

of our Lord, and thank God for eternal life, but total redemption is not yet ours. Not all enemies have been put under the feet of Christ. God will not rest nor will man be satisfied until reconciliation is total. We are God's stewards to help bring this about. The steward of God is interested in the perfecting of the saints.

As long as hunger, sickness, war, hate, injustice, selfishness, and death exist, God's purposes remain unfulfilled. Not until all things in heaven and on earth are gathered together in Christ, not until all tears are wiped away with no more death, sorrow, crying, or pain, and not until unbelief, hatred, immorality, lying, and corruption are cast out will the purposes of God be fulfilled.

Summary of God's Purposes

1. God is concerned about His created world. Before man was created God looked upon His creation and declared it good. But "there was not a man to till the ground." Because of His concern for creation God said, "Let us make man in our image . . . and let them have dominion." Man was to be God's steward in caring for this earth and having dominion over it. In other words, man was to promote God's interests in the earth. This is man's stewardship today. However, it includes much more in today's world than it did in the garden before the Fall.

God created a good earth with fertile soil, fresh waters, and pure air — an abundance of natural resources. Good stewardship on the part of God's people demands that they utilize these resources. They are to conserve and care for God's world and His creatures. God's people are to be responsible stewards of this earth.

2. Since the Fall God's great concern has been man's redemption, the restoration to his former glory. Christ came to seek and save lost man. He expects His redeemed

people to be His stewards in making disciples of all nations. We are to be His witnesses to the ends of the earth. We are stewards of reconciliation and redemption.

3. God's purpose for man is more than receiving Christ and being justified by faith. The sanctification and the glorification of man is also God's will. He wants man to conform to the image of His Son. A major task of God's stewards today is "perfecting the saints for the work of the ministry." We must help people grow in grace and become mature persons. Paul considered it his task not only to go to the unsaved with the gospel, but also to return and establish churches and build up and strengthen the believers. We are God's stewards in promoting the sanctification of believers.

4. God's purpose includes not only the spiritual but also the physical and mental welfare of His people. Repeatedly in the Old Testament He asked His people to provide for the poor, the orphans, the widows, and the foreigners. Often the prophets rebuked Israel for neglecting the needy. Jesus was concerned for the hungry, the sick, the lepers, the blind, and the oppressed. He sent out His disciples to preach the gospel of the kingdom, to heal the sick, cleanse the lepers, raise the dead, cast out devils, and freely give. When as stewards we do not include physical wholeness and mental health, as well as spiritual rebirth, the gospel becomes fragmented.

At this point Jesus' teaching on stewardship of possessions is so relevant. Repeatedly He taught that one could lay up treasures in heaven by using his possessions compassionately to meet the needs of people. On Judgment Day those on the left will be cast out because they did not minister to the needy.

One day a young lawyer came to Jesus and asked how he could inherit everlasting life. To justify himself he asked, "Who is my neighbor?" Jesus told him the story of the Good Samaritan and asked who was neighbor to the one who fell among thieves. The lawyer replied, "The one who showed mercy." Jesus told him to go and do the same. In answer to the question, "How is it possible for me to inherit eternal life?" Jesus said, "Show compassion like the Samaritan did." Jesus taught the same truth in the parables of the rich man and Lazarus and the unforgiving servant, and in the accounts of Zacchaeus and the rich young ruler.

Menno Simons said, "True evangelical faith can not be dormant, it clothes the naked, it feeds the hungry, it comforts the sorrowful, it shelters the destitute, it serves those who harm it, it binds up that which is wounded, it has become all things to men."

Practical Ways of Promoting God's Purposes

In the first three chapters of Ephesians, Paul has shown us what God has done, what He is doing, and what He will yet do for us. His eternal purpose is that we should live to the praise of His glory.

In the last three chapters he gives practical suggestions for fulfilling that purpose. We are living to the praise of His glory when we walk worthy of our calling, in lowliness, meekness, patience, forbearing one another in love, eager to maintain the Spirit in the bond of peace. We need to equip ourselves for the work of the ministry and for building the body of Christ. We praise His glory when we attain to the unity of the faith, to mature manhood, to the measure of the stature of the fullness of Christ, and when we avoid the excesses and sins of the ungodly. We live to the praise of His glory when we have right family and social relationships and when we are strong in the Lord and wear the whole armor of God.

Progression of God's Purposes

God's purpose to prepare a people has been advancing steadily from the beginning. Progressively God showed His people what His will was. From the time of Adam to the present God desired that His people be co-laborers with Him to carry out His work on earth. In the beginning this responsibility meant caring for and developing God's creation and having fellowship with the Creator.

Later stewardship meant being loyal citizens of the Hebrew nation, promoting the welfare of God's people. They were to be witnesses to the nations, to support the priesthood and the temple, attend the religious festivals, love God and keep His commandments. It meant being the people of God and ministering to the needs of His people.

In the New Testament stewardship means becoming members of the body of Christ, the new Israel, loyally supporting and promoting the work of Christ through His church. It means reconciling the world to God, perfecting the saints, and ministering to the needs of God's people. Stewardship always means using God-given resources to promote God's will in preparing a community of faith and love, a people who would reflect God's love and holiness.

5

STEWARDS
OF GOD

"This is how men should regard us, as servants of Christ
and stewards of the mysteries of God. Moreover, it is required of stewards that they be trustworthy" (1 Cor.
4:1, 2).

When we consider the holiness, the majesty, and the
perfection of God and when we think of His grand and
benevolent purposes in the world, what manner of persons
should we as His stewards be? The great desire of God
for His people is that they be like Him.

God is glorified only as His character is recognized
by and reflected in His people. He wanted Israel to be
witnesses of His glory and power among the nations. He
punished them for profaning His name. "Thus says the
Lord God: It is not for your sake, O house of Israel, that
I am about to act, but for the sake of my holy name,
which you have profaned among the nations to which you
came. And I will vindicate the holiness of my great name
. . . which you have profaned" (Ezek. 36:22, 23).

As Christians we too are a chosen race, a royal
priesthood, God's own people, to declare the wonderful
deeds of Him who called us out of darkness into His

marvelous light (1 Pet. 2:9). We are to be imitators of
God, as beloved children. We are to "walk in love, as
Christ loved us and gave himself up for us" (Eph. 5:1, 2).

The Cause of Man's Failure

Even though man was created in God's image, to promote His purposes and to be trustees of His creation, man
was not satisfied to be a steward; he wanted to be like
God. Man had not only an improper concept of the Creator
and an inadequate concept of the good purposes of God,
but he had also a distorted concept of himself. Because of
his pride and egotism man has become self-centered.
Everything orbits about man. He exploits God's world for
his own selfish purposes, disregards and misuses his fellow
creatures, and fails to render to God what is His. His own
selfish interests and pleasures have become his highest
good.

Too often Christian theology has tended to promote
this kind of distortion and this man-centeredness. While it
is true that man is the crown of God's creation, God also
cares for the rest of His creatures and His world. We are
inclined to interpret John 3:16 that God so loved mankind.
But the world God loved included more than man. No
doubt man was primary, but the redemption of the world
was wrapped up in man's redemption.

When God lost man He lost the world that He had
placed under man's dominion. He lost the silver and the
gold; He lost the cattle on a thousand hills; He lost the
farms and the forests. These must be brought back in
right relationship with God, and this happens only as man
is redeemed, not only spiritually, but socially, economically,
and in every area of his life.

Church treasuries suffer, missions lag, and the hungry
starve because farms, businesses, and wealth have not yet

been fully redeemed. They are dependent on man's redemption. "The transformation of the universe depends upon the completion of man's transformation by the working of God's grace" (Tyndale, *New Testament Commentary*, Rom. 8:18-30).

Worldly Stewards Versus Christian Stewards

In one sense all God's created beings are His stewards, whether voluntary or involuntary. God created all to promote His glory and His will. In spite of their rebellion and disobedience men still serve His purposes. God uses wicked men and nations to promote His kingdom. He used the Chaldeans, a wicked and violent nation, to punish His people (Hab. 1:6). He used Cyrus, King of Persia, to rebuild the temple (2 Chron. 36:2). He used Pharaoh to bring glory to His name (Ex. 9:16). God overruled the cruel acts of Joseph's brethren to accomplish His will (Gen. 50:20). "Surely the wrath of man shall praise thee" (Ps. 76:10).

Paul tells us in Romans 13 that earthly rulers are ministers of God, executing punishment on evildoers. God used Jewish officials, in spite of their malicious and evil intentions, to bring about the crucifixion of Christ and our redemption.

Twice in the Book of Job the sons of God presented themselves before the Lord. On both occasions Satan met with them and presented himself (1:6; 2:1). He received instructions from God. He will continue to serve God's purposes in a sinful world until both sin and Satan are cast out.

However, the involuntary contributions of the enemies of God will not be accompanied by joy or reward. Only doom awaits them. They are not motivated by gratitude, self-giving, or love, but by self-love, envy, and pride.

The Christian steward, on the other hand, is a voluntary servant of God. By free choice he has received Christ and become a son of God. By the Spirit he has been baptized into Christ's body. Being free from the law of sin and death he walks after the Spirit and not after the flesh. He willingly uses all his resources to promote God's kingdom.

Two Open Hands

The Christian steward has both hands wide open. One hand is open to receive God's grace — forgiveness, cleansing, salvation, abundant life, and assurance. He has experienced the peace of God, and the love of God has flooded his heart. His other hand, the giving hand, is also wide open as he administers God's gifts and shares them with others.

Only as we open our receiving hand can we open our giving hand. Everything we have comes from God. As we receive His gifts we can share them. However, when the giving hand is closed the receiving hand also closes. This is true in the matter of forgiveness. God says that if we do not forgive, we will not be forgiven; if we forgive, we will be forgiven. If our giving hand is open to forgive our brother, our receiving hand will be open and we receive forgiveness from God. If we close the giving hand and do not forgive, the receiving hand will be closed also.

This is true also in love and service. If the giving hand is open freely bestowing love and service, the receiving hand will be open to receive the blessings of God. If we do not love and serve we will not receive the blessings God wants to give us.

The same thing applies in regard to possessions. When Israel had the giving hand open and generously gave of their tithes and offerings they were blessed with prosperity. Whenever their giving hand was closed and they robbed God of tithes and offerings they found themselves in poverty. God challenged them to open the giving hand and see if the receiving hand would not open also.

Paul says the same thing. "He who sows sparingly will also reap sparingly, and he who sows bountifully will also reap bountifully." Paul is saying that if the giving hand is only partly open the receiving hand will also be only partly open; if the giving hand is wide open the receiving hand will also be wide open. Many Christian stewards have experienced this truth. The Christian steward is receptive to the gifts of God and is generous in sharing them.

The Steward Must Be a Dedicated Person

The true steward of God has presented his body a living sacrifice, holy and acceptable to God. There is a picture of an ox standing between a yoke and an altar with the inscription, "Ready for either." That represents the loyal steward of God. He is ready to live or ready to die for his Lord.

As a lad in North Dakota, I walked down the aisle of our church in response to an invitation given by the evangelist. That was a great day in my life; I was consciously dedicating myself to God. He accepted that sacrifice.

Years later a man of God who influenced my life greatly, and a man for whom I thank God, presented a challenge for persons to dedicate themselves to full-time Christian service. Again I walked forward and placed myself on the altar of service. God also accepted that sacrifice. That day perhaps marked the greatest change in my life. It gave me a sense of stewardship which I had never had and which I have never lost.

It is unfortunate that invitations like that are not

given today in many of our churches. Public dedication of one's life in the presence of God's people can be a tremendous motivation and blessing and a challenge to others.

What would it mean if farmers and businessmen would walk down the aisles of their churches and say, "I am dedicating myself, my farm, or my business, to God"? The great purposes of God are being hindered for lack of this kind of dedication.

Some years ago I heard of a college president who prayed something as follows: "Lord, the cattle on a thousand hills are yours. Won't you please sell a carload of them to pay off the college debt?" It seemed like a strange prayer to pray, but was it? Some time later he received a letter from a rancher with a check enclosed. The letter ran something as follows: "I have sold some of my cattle and was led to give a carload to the Lord's work and felt impressed to send it to your institution." Stewards of God should constantly be doing things like this. Thank God for those who are. Not only should our bodies be dedicated, but also our time, talents, and possessions. Am I really dedicated to God if my pocketbook isn't? If my farm or business is not? Stewardship means total dedication.

The Steward of God Must Be Trustworthy

"It is required of stewards that they be found trustworthy." Why did God call Abraham to be the father of His people? Because he was trustworthy. "For I know him, that he will command his children and his household after him." Joseph was made steward of all that Potiphar had because he was trustworthy. Only when he was slandered and Potiphar was led to believe he was not faithful was he discharged and imprisoned.

In the parable of the talents the trustworthy stewards

63

were promoted while the one who was not trustworthy was demoted (Mt. 25). In Luke 16 Jesus gives the parable of the unfaithful steward. His lord called him and said, "How is it that I hear this of thee? . . . thou mayest be no longer steward." This man, like Adam and Eve, when found untrustworthy was relieved of his responsibilities.

Jesus said to His disciples, "Who then is that faithful and wise steward, whom his lord shall make ruler over his household, to give them their portion of meat in due season? Blessed is that servant, whom his lord when he cometh shall find so doing. Of a truth I say unto you, that he will make him ruler over all that he hath" (Lk. 12:42-44). God's stewards must be trustworthy.

The Steward Is Accountable to God

"So each of us shall give account of himself to God" (Rom. 14:12). As stated elsewhere Daniel Webster once said that the most serious thought that ever entered his mind was his accountability to God. After Adam had disobeyed God he was called to account, "Where are you? . . . Have you eaten of the tree of which I commanded you not to eat?" After Cain had slain his brother, God confronted him with the question, "Where is Abel your brother?"

In Malachi, God calls Israel to account for their unfaithfulness, "And I will come near to you in judgment; and I will be a swift witness against the sorcerers, and against the adulterers, and against false swearers, and against those that oppress the hireling in his wages, the widow, and the fatherless, and that turn aside the stranger from his right, and fear not me, saith the Lord" (3:5). Not only must they give account for oppressing the hireling, the widow, and the fatherless, but also for robbing God of tithes and offerings.

The accountability of God's stewards is shown graphically in the parable of the judgment of the nations. Those who failed to use their resources for God's purposes, compassionately ministering to others, were accused of neglecting Christ Himself. They were asked to depart into everlasting fire prepared for the devil and his angels. On the other hand, those who had been faithful stewards, using their resources to promote God's will and ministering to others, were called blessed and invited to inherit the kingdom.

Charles Wesley was conscious of his accountability to God when he wrote:

"Arm me with zealous care,
As in Thy sight to live;
And O! Thy servant, Lord, prepare
A strict account to give.

"Help me to watch and pray,
And on Thyself rely;
Assured, if I my trust betray,
I shall forever die."

The Steward Should Be a Joyful Person

God's community is to be a joyous community. In His presence is fullness of joy, and at His right hand pleasures forever more (Ps. 16:11). Jesus said to His followers, "I have told you this so that you can share my joy, and that your happiness may be complete" (Jn. 15:11, Phillips). Christians dishonor God when they go around with long faces and constantly express their pessimism. Even under persecution Christ's followers are to rejoice and be exceedingly glad.

David asked his choir to sing, "Let the heavens be glad, and let the earth rejoice: and let men say among

65

the nations, The Lord reigneth. . . . Let the fields rejoice, and all that is therein. Then shall the trees of the
wood sing out at the presence of the Lord" (1 Chron.
16:31-33). Not only did God want a community of love
and joy; He wanted all of creation to be joyful. "Bless
the Lord, all his works in all places of his dominion: bless
the Lord, O my soul" (Ps. 103:22).

"Sing, O heavens; and be joyful, O earth; and break
forth into singing, O mountains!" [1]

Many of the psalms exhort us to be joyful and praise
the Lord. A favorite expression of Jesus was "Be of good
cheer." When His disciples were storm-tossed, He told
them to be of good cheer. He told the sick man to be of
good cheer. He told His disciples when persecuted to "be
of good cheer." When we are in danger, when we are ill,
when we are persecuted, we are to rejoice. Joy does not
depend on outward circumstances. When we have the
Lord of joy in our hearts, the joy of the Lord is ours.

Paul said, "Rejoice in the Lord alway: and again I
say Rejoice" (Phil. 4:4). He also said, "Rejoice ever-
more" (1 Thess. 5:16).

With strife, violence, poverty, and suffering in the
world, we as Christians must resist the tendency to become despondent. While these things should cause us real
concern, we must not let them rob us of the joy of the
Lord. We must deal with sin and suffering at the foot of
the mountain. We must never lose sight of the victory and
the glory at the top of the mountain. The great purposes of God will be fulfilled; He will have a community
of justice, love, and joy. Since we are stewards in promoting such a community, we should reflect the joy of
the Lord. John Ruskin said, "We may be sure, whatever we are doing, that we cannot be pleasing to Him
if we are unhappy ourselves."

Joy and Christian Giving

Joyful people will be generous people, and generous people will be joyful people. It is difficult to say which is cause and which is effect. Either one produces the other. The joy of the Macedonians caused an overflow of giving to others. 2 Cor. 8:2. After Israel had given generously for building the temple, "Then the people rejoiced, for that they offered willingly . . . to the Lord" (1 Chron. 29:9).

The reason some people give grudgingly is not because they are poor, but because they are not grateful and they lack the joy of the Lord. When we are grateful and joyful, we will have a sincere desire to give to Christ's kingdom and help to meet the needs of people. The poor people of Macedonia who were full of joy begged for the opportunity to give to the needs of the Christians at Jerusalem. Paul told the Corinthians that God loves the person who is happy when he gives.

The Christian steward should cultivate the fruit of the Spirit, which includes love and joy. He should help promote a community of joy because that is the will of his Lord. A revival of gratitude and praise among our people would bring with it a revival of generous giving. Conversely, a revival of generous giving would increase the joy of God's people.

The sources of joy are with us if we but tap them — the joy of salvation, the joy of Christian fellowship, the joy of the Spirit's presence, the joy of peace and love in our hearts, the joy of our glorious hope! But we permit them to lie dormant — we fail to express them, to witness, to praise, and to celebrate. These joys are unreal because we do not exercise them; we live as though they were not there; we deny them.

To be overdemonstrative is a danger, but a greater danger to most of us is the lack of praise, thanksgiving, and celebration. Incidentally, these things could substantially increase our offerings. The grateful, joyous person will be a generous person.

The Steward of God Is a Person of Faith

"For giving is a matter of faith. It is rooted at the heart of the Christian gospel and our response to that gospel." [2] One of the greatest obstacles to good stewardship is a lack of faith. People do not really believe that it is more blessed to give than to receive. They are not sure that if they seek first the kingdom other things will be added; not sure that the windows of heaven will be opened if they render tithes and offerings. They have doubts that the debt can be paid off or that they can balance the budget if they take ten percent from their paychecks.

We are somewhat deists, believing that God has separated Himself from the material world and is interested only in the spiritual realm. We feel it would lower the dignity of God to increase crops, help us to better jobs, increase our wages, or give us better health. This kind of unbelief hinders faithful stewardship.

Jesus rebuked this type of unbelief. He rebuked the disciples because of their fear of the storm. He was with them and He controls storms. At the foot of the mountain Jesus rebuked the disciples for lack of faith to heal the epileptic. God's power includes power over disease and sickness. In the Sermon on the Mount Jesus tells us not to worry about food, drink, and clothing. God feeds the birds and clothes the lilies. Will He not much more feed and clothe us? If we seek first the kingdom, these things will be supplied by the Father.

Faith is the lever that joins us to the infinite power of God. It was faith that caused Abel to offer a greater sacrifice than Cain. It was by faith that Enoch could walk with God and please Him in the midst of a corrupt society. By faith Noah believed and obeyed God, heeding God's warning of "things not seen as yet." Faith prompted Abraham to sacrifice his son, believing that God would raise him from the dead. By faith Moses rejected the splendor and riches of Egypt, "esteeming the reproach of Christ greater riches than the treasures in Egypt."

Through faith others subdued kingdoms, wrought righteousness, stopped the mouths of lions, quenched the violence of fire. All of these were faithful stewards of God because they believed God and that He is a rewarder of them that diligently seek Him.

That kind of faith has inspired men and women to dedicate themselves, to give generously what seemed beyond their means, and to experience blessings far above expectations. A lack of this faith in God causes a retrenchment in missions and a lack of funds for the promotion of God's purposes and for meeting the needs of the suffering people of the world. "Without faith it is impossible to please" God.

The Steward Is a Grateful Person

Gratitude is one of the great Christian virtues. The grateful person is a happy person; the ungrateful person cannot be a happy person. The grateful person will be a generous person, while the ungrateful person will not.

Paul tells the Colossians that if they have been raised with Christ they should seek the things above, not the things of the earth. He mentions a number of things the one raised with Christ will put off and certain virtues he will put on. Col. 3. In verse 15 he says, "And let the peace of God rule in your hearts . . . and be ye thankful." In the next verse, "Let the word of Christ dwell in you richly" and "sing psalms and hymns and spiritual songs with thankfulness in your hearts to God." And in verse 17, "And whatever you do, in word or deed, do everything in the name of the Lord Jesus, giving thanks to God and the Father through him."

In these three verses three times he exhorts us to be thankful. We will be a thankful people if we have the peace of Christ ruling in our hearts, if the word of Christ dwells in us richly, and if we are doing everything in the name of the Lord Jesus. This person will be a happy, generous steward of God. The Christian steward should cultivate and practice the grace of gratitude; he should be grateful to God, to his church, to society, and to his family. We need not look deeply to find occasion for gratitude.

God has forgiven our sins. Through Christ we have the abundant life. God has given us the Holy Spirit as a guarantee of our total redemption. He has given us the glorious hope of sharing His heavenly kingdom. He supplies all our needs and freely gives us all things. How can we but generously respond in gratitude to such love and grace? "Love so amazing, so divine, demands my soul, my life, my all."

When I lack total commitment to Jesus Christ, fail to gladly use my talents in furthering the work of His kingdom, or when I refuse to render tithes and offerings and share generously my possessions to promote the great purposes of God, I am most certainly demonstrating my lack of gratitude to God. The true steward is a grateful person. He will endeavor to promote gratitude among the people of God. He wants a grateful community.

The Christian Steward Is Inspired by Hope

The Christian's hope is a dynamic motivation to faithful stewardship. This hope was the basis of Abraham's faithfulness, "For he looked for a city which hath foundations, whose builder and maker is God." Moses forsook the wealth of Egypt for "he looked to God for his reward." The men and women in Hebrews were spurred on by hope, "These all died in faith, not having received the promises, but having seen them afar off, and were persuaded of them, and embraced them. . . . But now they desire a better country, that is, an heavenly: wherefore God is not ashamed to be called their God: for he hath prepared for them a city" (11:13-16).

Jesus was willing to die a shameful death on the cross because of the joy He knew would be His later (Heb. 12:2, *The Living Letters*). Paul could endure much suffering for the sake of Christ because of the hope of glory that would be revealed in him. Paul's letter to Titus exhorts Christians to deny ungodliness and worldly lusts and live righteously, "Looking for that blessed hope, and the glorious appearing of the great God and our Saviour Jesus Christ" (Tit. 2:12, 13).

Both Jesus and Paul use the blessed hope as an incentive for good stewardship — for sharing and giving possessions. Both refer to laying up treasures in heaven. The Christian with this hope before him can be sure that in giving and sharing he is making the best possible investment. Paul tells Timothy to charge the rich "that they do good, that they be rich in good works, ready to distribute, willing to communicate, laying up in store for themselves a good foundation against the time to come, that they may lay hold on eternal life" (1 Tim. 6:18, 19). The person who has this glorious hope and who has faith in God's great promises for the future will respond by dedication of self and possessions. He will want to be rich toward God with eternal treasures laid up in heaven. The faithful steward will keep before him that glorious hope.

Stewardship and a Right Relationship with God

Without a right relationship with God man will not be a good steward. Conversely, a man who is not a faithful steward is not right in his relationship with God. Faithful stewardship and right relationship with God are two sides of the same coin. God created man to be His steward. Faulty stewardship is an indication of faulty relationships.

When the disciples had prayed at Pentecost, the place was shaken where they were assembled. They were filled with the Holy Spirit, and they spake the word of God with boldness. "And the multitude of them that believed were of one heart and of one soul: neither said any of them that ought of the things which he possessed was his own; but they had all things common. And with great power gave the apostles witness of the resurrection of the Lord Jesus: and great grace was upon them all" (Acts 4:32, 33).

The writer of Acts also says that none lacked. Those who possessed houses or lands sold them and brought the prices of the things sold and laid them at the apostles' feet. Distribution was made according to need. Right relationship with God resulted in stewardship of the gospel and stewardship of possessions.

We notice that the same thing happened to Zacchaeus as recorded in Luke 19. When he had met Jesus and "salvation had come to his house," he declared, "Behold, Lord, the half of my goods I give to the poor; and if I have taken any thing from any man by false accusation, I restore him fourfold." Conversion, right relationship with the Lord, affected his life and pocketbook.

Man's One Major Problem

Someone has said that man basically has but one major problem and all others are secondary. That problem is

72

God's relationship to man and man's relationship to God. When the major problem is solved correctly, other things will fall into place. If not, all else will be disjointed, aimless, and drifting.

If man were in right relationship with God wars would cease and men would live in peace. If all members of the Christian church were in perfect relationship with their Maker the hungry people of the world would be fed and the world would be evangelized. The Christian brotherhood would then be the community of love, peace, righteousness, and reconciliation that God in His eternal wisdom willed it to be.

Right relationship with God means doing the will of God by using the resources He has given us to fulfill His purposes. We dare not misuse or use selfishly our abilities or our possessions. We cannot spend large amounts of money selfishly on luxuries and pleasures, contributing little to the church and to the needy. We will not permit retrenchment in missions for lack of funds while we ourselves are living in a state of affluence.

In the face of the great needs of the world can we really call Jesus "Lord" while giving only 2 percent or 5 percent of our income to meet these needs when our average income exceeds that of three fourths of the people of the world? Is not this indifference to the world's needs and lack of commitment to the church of Christ a true indication of lack of commitment to Christ and of an inadequate relationship with God? Can we call Him "Lord, Lord" and not do what He wills for us to do?

Faulty stewardship is surely a sign of an improper relationship with God. Empty church treasuries in a society of affluence unmistakably indicate inadequate relationship with our Lord. They result in retrenchment of missions and in curtailment of benevolent services.

Man Longs for Right Relationship with God

John declared, "Beloved, now are we the sons of God." The psalmist said, "We are his people, and the sheep of his pasture." While the Apostle Paul expresses this relationship, "And ye are Christ's; and Christ is God's. Let a man so account of us as of the ministers of Christ and the stewards of the mysteries of God." What a blessed relationship redeemed man has with his Creator! We are His children, His sheep, His people, His stewards. This is the relationship for which he was created and for which fallen man yearns.

Job voiced this yearning of the world when he cried, "Oh that I knew where I might find him." The psalmist likewise expressed that universal craving when he cried out, "As the hart panteth after the water brooks, so panteth my soul after thee, O God. My soul thirsteth for God." Saint Augustine declared, "Our souls are not at rest until they find rest in Thee, O God." Man was created for a sonship, a stewardship relationship with God, and is never satisfied outside that relationship.

Man has always been inclined to turn from God and to seek satisfying relationships elsewhere. But his efforts to find it always meet with futility and frustration. God says, "My people have committed two evils: they have forsaken me the fountain of living waters, and hewed them out cisterns, broken cisterns, that can hold no water" (Jer. 2:13).

Millions of thirsty people today instead of drinking at the fountain of living waters are trying to satisfy their thirst from broken cisterns of the world that can hold no water. Many are flocking to materialism, spiritism, hippyism, worldly pleasures, and other false gods in futile attempts to find meaning in life, to find identity, to relate to reality.

While in India in 1963 I saw many Hindus in deep devotion present offerings and bow to gods of stone, bathe themselves in sacred waters, and bow before the sacred cow. They were seeking relationship with the Divine. But the broken cisterns of Hinduism could not quench their thirst.

After I had preached one night in the city of Madras a high caste Hindu, a Brahman, asked to speak to me. He said that for 30 years he had been studying philosophy and religion. He said, "I have now come to the place that I accept Jesus Christ as the only God. Even though I am a Hindu I have a great peace in my heart." As I talked and prayed with him I sensed that I was speaking to one who had drunk from the fountain of living waters and the thirst for relationship with God was satisfied. What the broken cisterns of philosophy and religion could not do the water which Christ gives did for him.

When one truly knows the Lord and has found a satisfying relationship with Him, he gladly dedicates himself to spend and be spent for his Lord. Like Paul he will say, "Yea, woe is unto me, if I preach not the gospel! . . . I am made all things to all men, that I might by all means save some." [3]

6

STEWARDSHIP
OF LIFE

"Have you forgotten that your body is the temple of the Holy Spirit, who lives in you, and is God's gift to you, and that you are not the owner of your body? You have been bought, and at what a price! Therefore bring glory to God in your body" (1 Cor. 6:19, 20, Phillips).

God breathed into man the breath of life and made him a person. As stewards we must recognize that we are stewards of life, a trust from God. We must seek to glorify God in our bodies. We should dedicate life with all its powers to God's glory and to the promotion of His kingdom.

Stewardship of Personality

God wants His people to be His witnesses, to be lights in the world, to be the salt of the earth, "mature men reaching the height of Christ's full stature." This goal calls for strong, well-integrated personalities. God created man in His image, crowned him with glory and honor, and gave him a perfect personality. After the image was marred by sin, God desired to restore man to his former glory.

Human personality is of supreme worth to God. The Ten Commandments, the teaching of Scripture, and the atonement are for man's restoration. They enhance and perfect his personality, and make him into the image of the Son. The things that mar man's personality are rebuked and forbidden. God admonishes us to grow in Christlikeness and to abstain from fleshly lusts that war against us.

Physical, mental, and moral traits help make up this intangible something we call "personality." Well-developed bodies, disciplined intellects, emotional stability, properly developed instincts or biological drives contribute to well-integrated personalities. God asks His people to be strong, to put on the whole Christian armor, to bear the fruit of the Spirit, and to grow in grace. He wants His people to be workmen that need not be ashamed.

We Are Stewards of Our Bodies

"And so, dear brothers, I plead with you to give your bodies to God. Let them be a living sacrifice, holy — the kind he can accept" (Rom. 12:1, *The Living Bible*).

What wonderful bodies God has given us; we are "fearfully and wonderfully made." God permits us to live in these bodies, but He also wants them for His temple. To take the attitude, "This body is mine; I can do what I want to with it," is wrong. To ruin this body by the use of alcohol, narcotics, vice, and sin is destroying and defiling God's temple. We should recognize that our bodies are the temples of the Holy Spirit. Thus we ought to develop clean, strong, and useful bodies for His glory and for service to our fellowmen.

In a tract entitled, "Whose Body Is Yours?" the late Dr. Walter Wilson of Kansas City tells how zealous for the Lord he was when first converted. He distributed tracts and did personal work, yet his life seemed to be empty — there were no results. One evening he heard an evangelist speak on Romans 12:1. He asked, "To whom shall I yield my body? To Christ, the Son. No, He has a body of His own. But the Holy Spirit has no body. He wants to dwell in my body, and use my body." Walter Wilson went home deeply under conviction. He threw himself on the floor and prayed, "Holy Spirit, I have sinned against You. I have acted as though this body were mine. From now it is Your body, do what You want with it. You may send it to the hospital with cancer or send it to Africa as a missionary. It is Your body." Peace came to his soul. He went to bed and slept.

Before going to work the next morning he said to his wife, "You may hear from me today. Before this I thought this body was mine, but I have dedicated it to the Holy Spirit and I believe He is going to use it." Shortly after he arrived at the office two girls came in. They had often come before · to get advertisements for the local paper. But this morning Dr. Wilson's body was dedicated to the Spirit. The Spirit, through Dr. Wilson's lips, greeted the girls, "Good morning, girls. Are you bad enough to be lost this morning?" The older one broke down and said, "I am. For a long time I have been wanting someone to point me to Christ." It was an easy matter to lead her to the Lord. The younger girl took the attitude, "I'm not a bad girl," but the Spirit used Dr. Wilson to show her the need in her life. Both girls left the office with Christian assurance because Dr. Wilson had yielded his body to the Spirit. Throughout his life the Spirit used Walter Wilson in a marvelous way in blessing the lives of many people. He was a good steward of his body and of his life.

In Romans 6 Paul tells us to be good stewards of the members of our bodies. We must not yield them as instruments unto sin, but yield them to God as instruments of righteousness. What does he mean? He means that as Christians we should not permit our feet to take us to dens of vice or walk in the way of the ungodly. We should guide our feet in the paths of truth, righteousness, and service.

Our hands must not be instruments of wrongdoing and violence, but be used in doing good, serving others, and doing the work of the Lord. Our eyes should not look upon and our ears should not listen to that which defiles, but attend to what is pure, noble, and good. This may sometimes mean turning off or changing channels on our radios and TVs. We should not permit our lips to engage in gossip, slander, and evil speaking, but let them be instruments in witnessing for our Lord, singing the praises of God, and edifying our brothers in Christ. Our minds are not to think upon that which is impure, dishonest, and evil, but upon that which is pure, just, and holy.

We are stewards of the members of our bodies and are responsible for their proper use. We will be judged for tongues that use deceit, eyes that look upon the lustful, feet that run to mischief, and hands stained by theft and bribery. Our members should become powerful instruments of righteousness in promoting the great purposes of God.

Our bodies are the transmitters of the gospel of the kingdom. In 1930 King George of England was to give an important message at the opening of the London Naval Conference. The message was to be broadcast and the American people wanted to hear that message. It was to be rebroadcast by the Columbia Broadcasting Company. A few minutes before the message was to be given the young man at the controls at CBS discovered a broken wire. To call a repairman to repair it would take 20 minutes. By that time the American people would have missed most of the king's message. Without hesitation Walter Vivan grasped the ends of the broken wire and holding them together restored the broken connection. The shock of 250 volts, and the leakage of the current, caused his arms to twitch and burned his hands. But he held on at the peril of his life as the king's message went through.

The King of kings has an urgent message that our world sorely needs, but the connections have been broken by sin. Unless we are willing to take hold of the broken connections and let His message flow through us, the lost world will never hear it.

Stewards of the Soul

"For what good is it for a man to gain the whole world at the price of his own soul? What could a man offer to buy back his soul once he had lost it?" (Mt. 16:26, Phillips).

Here is one of the greatest stewardship questions ever asked. I am aware that many versions use the word "life" instead of soul. That is consistent with the translation of the Greek word in verse 25. However, a careful study of the context should convince one that the meaning is far more than mere physical life. In a parallel passage Luke says "loses himself," which certainly means much more than earthly life. Verse 24 suggests earthly life must be sacrificed for the sake of gaining eternal life. Verses 27 and 28 refer to Christ coming in judgment. It would seem that *The Living Bible* may be correct in translating it "and lose eternal life."

The greatest failure anyone can make in any area of stewardship is to fail to gain eternal life. The rich fool evidently was a great success in filling his barns, but he was the most miserable of stewards, exchanging eternal life for "things." By worldly standards the rich man, at whose gate lay poor Lazarus, was a success. He was clothed in purple and fine linen, and fared sumptuously every day. But "in hell he lifted up his eyes, being in torments." Another example of wretched stewardship! He neglected his own best welfare and missed the opportunity of ministering to his Lord. He was utterly unprepared to meet God. He missed the blessings of sharing and helping others. He was unconcerned about the glory of God and His great purposes.

"A charge to keep I have, a God to glorify;

A never-dying soul to save, and fit it for the sky."

This charge must receive high priority in the life of any steward. Not until we are in right relationship with God can we be good stewards in ministering to others or in advancing the kingdom of God.

We Are Stewards of Our Minds

"If you believe in goodness and if you value the approval of God, fix your minds on whatever is true and honorable and just and pure and lovely and praiseworthy" (Phil. 4:8, Phillips).

What tremendous powers God entrusted to man when He gave him his mental abilities. He has given man the powers of reason, judgment, imagination, memory; power to invent, plan, and execute, to have dominion over God's creation; power to build or to destroy; power to dominate or to serve. The mind of man has been able to accomplish great things. It has been able to overcome the obstacles of space and to place man on the moon. Man has made tremendous strides in medicine and science. He has been able to make kidney and heart transplants. He has split the atom, making available frightening power. He has invented machines that can exceed the speed of sound.

What a world man could have built had he been a good steward of his mental powers and used them for the

81

purposes of God. But, alas! man has not been a good steward; he has selfishly used these powers. The mind that should have built a peaceful world has instead built a world of war and bloodshed. The mind that should have built a world where poverty is unknown has instead built a world where the wealth is in the hands of a few and the masses go to bed hungry. The mind that should have built a free world has instead built a world where multitudes are in slavery.

Today keen minds that should be building better hospitals and medical services, conquering dreadful diseases, promoting a better way of life are instead working day and night to develop more deadly weapons of destruction. The good steward will use his God-given powers to develop a better world, a community of love, righteousness, and peace. How tragic when great minds are used for destructive and selfish purposes, working against the God who gave them these powers when they could have used them for the good of mankind. Our mental powers were not given us to use for selfish or destructive purposes. Good stewardship demands that we use these powers to make ourselves better persons, our churches better churches, our communities better communities, and the world a better world.

Construction Kits

The Bible commentator, William Barclay, says that God does not give us completed lives. He gives us raw materials out of which to make life. He gives us a construction kit with instructions. "God gives us ourselves, with all our gifts and our abilities; He gives us the world, with all its beauty and bounty, and its resources; He gives us the people we live with; and He says to us, 'Out of all these things make a life that is worthwhile.'

"But you would never get your construction kits to

come out right unless you follow the instructions.

"So it is with life. God gives us the raw materials of life, and God gives us the instructions how to turn them into a real and worthwhile life. He gives us the law and His commandments in His book; He gives us the guidance of His Holy Spirit; He gives us Jesus to be both our example and our power.

"God has given us all we need to make a life; God has given us the rules and instructions to follow and has given us His Son to help us do the things we could never do ourselves, and to make the life we never could construct ourselves." [1]

We are stewards of God in using this construction kit and the instructions that God has given us.

Figure it out for yourself, my lad,
You've all that the greatest of men have had:
Two arms, two hands, two legs, two eyes,
And a brain to use if you would be wise,
With this equipment they all began,
So start from the top and say, "I can."

Look them over, the wise and the great,
They take their food from a common plate,
And similar knives and forks they use,
With similar laces they tie their shoes.
The world considers them brave and smart,
But you've all they had when they made their start.

You can triumph and come to skill,
You can be great if you only will.
You're well equipped for what fight you choose;
You have arms and legs and a brain to use,
And the man who has risen great deeds to do
Began his life with no more than you.
— Edgar A. Guest

A word of caution is perhaps in order here. This may

have the ring of self-sufficiency and lifting one's self by his bootstraps. The Christian steward will always realize his dependence upon God and will endeavor to improve and develop his personality and powers by the help of the Spirit.

Stewards of Instincts

William Barclay states, "Instinct is the raw material of life: and as with all raw material, everything depends on how you use it.
There is the instinct of acquisitiveness.
"We can use it to develop a wise and prudent independence, to support ourselves and our loved ones by our own efforts, to build up a home, and to save something for the future and for all the things that can easily happen; or we can use it to become a miser gloating over our possessions, always keeping and possessing, never sharing and giving.
There is the instinct of self-defense and self-protection.
"We can use it to seek wise safety and to avoid foolish recklessness; or we can use it to produce, within ourselves, a weak cowardice which will face nothing, and whose policy in life is to run away from things.
There is the instinct of sex.
"We can use it to ennoble life, to be in the closest and most perfect relationship with someone else; or we can use it to become kin to the beasts, and even to ruin life for ourselves and for other people. It can lead life to the greatest of joys and the deepest of tragedies.
There is the instinct of gregariousness, the instinct which makes us avoid loneliness and seek the company of others.
"We can use it to build up friendship, to develop fellowship, to enter the circle of those most dear; or we can use it in such a way that we are only happy when we

are one of a crowd, and that we are quite incapable of taking an independent stand and of being alone. We can use it in such a way that we are unhappy if we have nothing but our own company to enjoy.

There is the instinct of motherhood.

"We can use it to be the foundation of a home, to lead to one of the most perfect relationships in the world; or out of it we can make what someone has called smother-love, which saps the independence and stifles the life of the child.

"God gave us the raw material of life. The question is, what are we going to make out of it?" [2]

A proper and balanced development of these instincts, or biological urges, results in a strong integrated personality. Misusing or neglecting them can cause wrecked characters and ruined lives. Examples of this are the miser and the spendthrift, the coward and the daredevil, the prostitute and the homosexual, the drunkard and the glutton, a snob or a hermit. The purposes of the kingdom call for stewards with well-integrated personalities.

Stewardship of Affections and Emotions

Years ago at the Federal prison at Ft. Leavenworth I met a man who, in a fit of anger, struck a man a fatal blow. He had not intended to kill him, but in spite of that he was spending a large part of his life in prison. He failed to control his passions or to be a good steward of his emotions.

God has given to man the power to love and to hate, to rejoice or be sorrowful, to fear and to become angry. These powers call for faithful stewardship on the part of Christians. The proper development and use of these powers can be tremendous factors in the personality, the character, the influence, the usefulness, and success of a person. On the other hand, improper development and misuse of these powers can mean warped personalities, wrecked lives,and a curse to society.

All of these emotions have their place and are good if properly managed and used. We could not be strong persons without them. But too often men are not good stewards in the use of these powers but use them selfishly and against the will of God. They hate the wrong things and love what should be hated. Instead of being angry at dishonesty, injustice, and sin, they become angry at those who cross their paths. Instead of loving righteousness, truth, and holiness, they love sinful pleasures, the ways of the world. How wonderful it would be if everyone hated dishonesty, cheating, filthy conversation, lust, and sin; and if everyone's anger would be aroused by injustice, racism, hypocrisy, war, and evil.

The Scriptures, both the Old Testament and the New Testament, exhort the people of God to properly employ the powers of emotion. We are to love righteousness and hate iniquity; to love God and our fellowmen, even our enemies. We are to abhor what is evil and cleave to what is good. We are not to love the world, neither the things in the world. If we do not love our brothers, we are in darkness and do not know God. God's people also should cultivate the emotions of joy and sorrow. We are to rejoice with those who rejoice and weep with those who weep. We are to rejoice in the Lord always. God wants stewards of love, joy, and righteousness; stewards who hate evil, injustice, and things that defile and destroy.

Jesus and Anger

We may learn from Jesus, the Perfect Steward, about the use of emotions. What were the things that aroused His anger?

1. Jesus became angry with exploitation. This is shown in the cleansing of the temple (Jn. 2:15-17). Jesus saw the excessive rates that were being charged the poor pilgrims who had come to Jerusalem to worship. In anger He drove out the oxen and sheep and overturned the tables of the money changers.

2. His anger was kindled against those who loved tradition and religious systems more than people. He was angry with those who were so meticulous about Sabbath observance, yet unconcerned about the sick (Mk. 3:1-6).

3. Jesus was angry with hypocrisy. Time and again He rebuked the Pharisees for their hypocrisy and pronounced woes upon them. Seemingly, He was more tolerant with publicans and sinners than with hypocrites, people who said one thing with their lips and the opposite by their lives.

4. His parables show that He was angry with irresponsibility. Those who would not minister to people in distress were cast out (Mt. 25:41-45). In Luke we have the parable of the man who was sinfully rich, while at his gate was a desperately poor man. William Barclay commented that it was not what the rich man did that got him in jail; it was what he did not do that got him into hell.

The High Cost of Violating Stewardship Principles

God has graciously endowed man with the powers of personality, instincts, emotions, will, and mental abilities. These may be used for great good to man and for the purposes of God. They may be misused to man's hurt and against God's purposes. The law of stewardship has been instilled deeply in man and in God's creation. "The kingdom of God is within you." God's laws are written in our hearts, a part of our very being. Man was made for holiness, truth, purity, faith, and love. He was not made for unbelief, hatred, and evil. We were made to obey God's laws not to break them.

Our powers of personality were given to us to cooperate in the purposes of God and to obey His laws. E. Stanley Jones said, "We do not break the laws of God; they break us." When we break the law of love, we are in trouble — Vietnam, the Middle East, Watts, and Kent.

When we break the law of purity we really mess things up — broken homes, prostitution, venereal diseases of epidemic proportions, suffering, and death. Man has been made for God, for His laws, and for His purposes as the locomotive was made for the tracks. As long as the locomotive remains on the tracks it is free; when it leaves the tracks it loses its freedom.

Our bodies, minds, instincts, and emotions were made for right attitudes, right living, and for God's laws. We are to put on truth, love, mercy, and purity. These make for strength, character, and happiness. We are to put off lying, hatred, anger, envy, and lust. They hurt us physically, mentally, and spiritually. They mar Christian personality.

We are told by physicians that these may cause serious repercussions physically and mentally; they can affect the intestinal tract and slow or completely stop the process of digestion. A doctor said one should never eat when he is angry. A woman had vomiting spells, but her physician could find nothing wrong until he found that her mother-in-law, whom she hated, was coming for a visit. He advised the husband to wire his mother not to come. The vomiting stopped immediately. Another doctor was baffled by a baby's illness, until he heard the mother violently quarreling with her husband. He declared the mother was poisoning her child with her milk.

It is known that both the quality and the quantity of

a cow's milk may be affected by stress. I knew a dairyman who would not let strangers in his milking barn while he was milking his nervous Jersies. Another dairyman keeps his radio playing softly while the cows are being milked. A poultryman declared that after the Fourth of July, because of fire crackers and other noises, there were many more blood-spots in the ggs. Certain epidemics may break out in a flock of turkeys after they have been frightened by dogs or coyotes. God has written His laws deeply not only in man but also in His creation. Some people believe that even plants respond to kindness and violence.

Victims of hatred, anger, envy, and fear often pay dearly for it. An ophthalmologist said that he cannot examine the eyes of an angry man. Anger and resentment also can contribute to arthritis. A certain woman did not like her son-in-law who visited her every year. Whenever he arrived she suffered from arthritis. As soon as he left she was all right. Anxiety and resentments also contribute to stomach ulcers. Recently I read that when the Dow-Jones average skids the number of businessmen who have ulcers soars. Stomachs, nervous systems, physical structures were not made for hate, anger, lust, and fear but for good will, love, truth, righteousness, and faith.

"The kingdom of God is within you," said Jesus. Dr. Jung told a patient, "You are suffering from loss of faith in God and the future. Recover your faith and you will live. If you don't, you won't." Some physicians declare that 60 percent or more of the patients that come to them need a minister rather than a doctor.

The lusts of the flesh, the things the Scriptures tell us to mortify and put off, are sinful because they are hurtful. Hate, anger, anxiety, immorality, profanity, lying, and fear can wreck men physically, mentally, and spiritually. A lecturer told his audience that whenever a person uses profanity, poison is ejected into his system. The effect of intense rage and fear can be detected in both man and animals. Lying has a sufficient effect on man that it can be detected by machine. In LeTourneau's *Now*, August, 1972, the following appeared:

"Liars Snared Unawares"

"The Dektor Counter-intelligence and Security, Inc., has now a machine called the 'Psychological Stress Evaluator,' which is a new kind of lie detector! Lying produces stress and this machine works measuring the inaudible frequency modulations of the voice (along with the audible frequences) that are present under normal circumstances, but which disappear under stress."

We are partners with God in building strong, useful bodies, minds, personalities, and characters that conform to the image of His Son. When we use the raw materials He has entrusted to us and follow the instructions God gave us in His Word, we will develop into the people He wants us to be. We will be His stewards in preparing a people for the Lord.

Man's Temptation to Misuse God's Power

"God hath spoken once; twice have I heard this; that power belongeth unto God" (Ps. 62:11). God's power is limitless. The world is brimming over with His power; it is seen everywhere — in the sun, in the waterfalls, in the lightning and the winds, in the trees, in the minerals, and in the atom. In fact, all things material may be but a form of God's energy or power. One lecturer stated that there was enough power in one glass of water to drive the largest battleship across the ocean. A popular science monthly quoted Henry Ford as saying that there is enough power

in the alcohol made from an acre of potatoes to plow that
acre for a hundred years.

Great are the powers of God and He shares that power
with His stewards. He longs to enforce those powers by
the power of His Spirit. He makes it possible for us to be
strong in the Lord and in the power of His might when
we put on the whole armor of God. What could be accom-
plished by the people of God if they were good stewards
of their powers is beyond imagination! But from the beginning man has been inclined to use his resources selfishly. In this way he robs himself of power, hurts his
fellowmen, and works against the purposes of God.

Walt N. Johnson, in *Stewardship Vitalized*, suggests
four ways in which man misuses God's powers. [3]

1. Man uses power for selfish purposes, to get things
for himself. Many people spend most of their time, energy,
and money in pursuit of things to pamper their bodies.
When our bodies are our gods, the power of God will be
used, or abused, in lavishing things on self. Someone has
said that if we have something worthwhile to live for, it
does not take much to live on; but if we have little to
live for it takes a lot to live on. To use our powers to get
things is a gross violation of the stewardship of power.

2. Man uses power for display, or to gain attention.
He shows off at God's expense. He wants to make a name
for himself and have others adore him. Simon the sorcerer
offered money to the apostles for the power to do miracles.
Peter soundly rebuked him for wanting to use Holy Spirit
power to show off (Acts 8:18-25). The power that God entrusts to man should be used for God's glory, not man's.

Man is inclined to hail white power, black power,
youth power, and student power. If that is all these are,
we should not expect too much good to come from them.
Any one of them geared into God's power and used for

the purposes of God, in God's way of love and peace, could be a mighty force for good, but used selfishly they are futile. "Not by might, nor by power, but by my spirit, saith the Lord." Violence is not the way of the Christian steward; it is a misuse of God's power.

3. Man misuses power when he tries to rule his fellow-men. From earliest times man has been inclined to use his powers to enslave his fellowmen and use them for his purposes. Leaders of nations have built empires and great monuments with enslaved people. Solomon used his great powers to build a magnificent capitol but enslaved his people to do it. It resulted in the downfall of his kingdom and did not promote the purposes of God. Ecclesiastical leaders have not been free from misusing their powers to rule rather than to serve.

4. Man grossly misuses his power to maim and kill his fellowmen. This perhaps is a logical consequence of the other abuses of power mentioned above. When men use their powers selfishly, to show off and to rule, it is likely to escalate into bloodshed and slaughter. "From whence come wars and fightings among you? come they not hence, even of your lusts that war in your members?" (Jas. 4:1). As long as man uses power for selfish ends, there will be fightings and wars.

Think of the great power desecrated in the futile and brutal war in Vietnam. What those powers could have done if used for the purposes of God, in ministering to the needs and the advancement of man. What tragic loss of man-power, money-power, moral-power, and spiritual power!

In a report prepared for the Foreign Relations Committee of the U.S. Senate by the Foreign Affairs Division of Congressional Research Service the following statistics were given (as of the middle of 1971):

50,000 Americans killed.
300,000 Americans injured.
138,000 South Vietnam soldiers killed.
400,000 South Vietnam soldiers injured.
722,000 North Vietnam and Viet Cong soldiers killed.
325,000 South Vietnam civilians killed (estimate).
725,000 South Vietnam injured.
5,000,000 South Vietnam refugees, nearly one third of the population.
Approximately one seventh of land area of South Vietnam sprayed with chemical herbicides to reduce vegetation and destroy crops.
6.2 billion board feet of timber destroyed.
$120 billion spent at a time of serious poverty in the world.

"The kingdom of God is built on earth, not by force, but by testimony. . . . Force is use of power and touches only the secondary; it can destroy but never create; it deals with effects, not causes. It cannot reach the primary facts of life; it deals with bodies, never souls. It cannot win loyalty. It cannot teach. It cannot free. It cannot beget confidence. It cannot love, nor receive love. It cannot make people good." [4]

The Christian steward must be vitally concerned in building a strong, noble character and a well-integrated personality. He should seek to be the kind of person God wants His people to be, the person who reflects God's light, love, and righteousness. He will be concerned not to misuse his physical, intellectual, and spiritual powers, using them selfishly for destructive purposes. He will be God's steward in helping other people develop into Christ-like persons. He will be aware that he is his brother's keeper.

Stewards of God

AM I MY BROTHER'S KEEPER?

He stood at the crossroads all alone,
with the sunrise in his face;
He had no fear for the path unknown,
He was set for a manly race.
But the road stretched east, and the road stretched west;
There was no one to tell him which way was the best;
So my chum turned wrong and went down, down, down,
Till he lost the race and the victor's crown,
And fell at last in an ugly snare,
Because no one stood at the crossroads there.

Another chum on another day,
At the selfsame crossroads stood;
He paused a moment to choose the way
That would lead to the greater good.
And the road stretched east, and the road stretched west;
But I was there to show him the best;
So my chum turned right and went on and on,
Till he won the race and the victor's crown;
He came at last to the mansion fair,
Because I stood at the crossroads there.

Since then I have raised a daily prayer,
That I be kept faithfully standing there,
To warn the runners as they come,
And save my own and another's chum.
— Author unknown

7

STEWARDSHIP OF
GOD'S CREATION

Perhaps in no area of man's stewardship has he more flagrantly transgressed against God than in the care and preservation of His creation. The long-suffering Creator has long tolerated man's arrogance and his acts of outrage against His creatures and His creation, but man's sins are finding him out. With his unconcern for the rest of God's creation and with his insatiable desire to promote self and secure wealth, he has brought upon himself the "ecology crisis" which threatens his existence.

Many lay the blame of our dilemma at the door of Christianity with its anthropocentric ethic and theology, which encourage man to exploit and destroy the animals, the resources, and nature itself for his own selfish interests. Because of this fallacy in theology and ethics many, especially the youth, are turning to Zen Buddhism or Pantheism. But these philosophies cannot solve the ecological problem. They only inject new problems. Christians need to revise their system of ethics and theology to include not only man's relation to God and to man, but also to God's creatures and His creation.

Man must soon take a serious look at his responsibility

95

to his environment. If man is to survive on this planet, he must have a new concept of our Christian stewardship. Man's lack of concern for God's creation, his greed, and selfishness are making the earth an unfit place to live. A careful study of the Bible will show that God loves and is concerned about His world and wants us to have the same love and concern.

God's Concern for His Creation

We notice in the first chapters of Genesis that God's Spirit moved on the face of the waters. After each creative act, God saw that it was good. It was a good earth with a good atmosphere, good waters, good vegetation, and good animal life. God shows His concern for His creation in chapter 2, "And there was not a man to till the ground," no man to care for His world. God created man to care for the earth and to promote His purposes. Man was to till the soil, keep the garden, subdue the earth, and have dominion (1:28). This verse may be the root of some of our faulty ethics and theology. Man takes it as a blank check from God to exploit and misuse the animals, the forests, the soil, the waters, and the atmosphere. God never intended we do this.

God cares for His creation. He feeds the birds and clothes the lilies (Mt. 6:26-29). He notices the fall of the sparrow (Mt. 10:29, 30). He hears and feeds the animals (Ps. 104:21, 22; 145:16). He calls the stars by name (Ps. 147:4). He rejoices in what He creates (Is. 65:17, 18). God provides food for both man and every living thing. He gives to man the seeds of the herbs and the fruit of the trees. To the beasts, the birds, and every creeping thing God gives every green herb. There is total absence of any suggestion that animals and birds were to devour each other, or that man was to feast upon animals and birds.

Not until after the Flood was man told he could use animals for food.

All Creation Was Affected by Man's Fall

The result of man's disobedience in the garden had cosmic effects (Gen. 3:14-19). The serpent was cursed above all cattle, made to crawl on its belly and eat dust. The sorrow of the woman was multiplied and she was made subject to her husband. The ground was cursed for man's sake, and man's joy was turned to sorrow. Thorns and thistles would grow to plague man. Henceforth man would eat bread in the sweat of his face until he returned to the ground. Man was driven from a beautiful garden, lest he eat of the tree of life. Sin affected man's relationship not only with God, but also with man, and with the rest of God's creation.

In time these relationships worsened. Cain murdered his brother Abel. "God saw that the wickedness of man was great in the earth, and that every imagination of the thoughts of his heart was only evil continually" (Gen. 6:5). We see the growing breach between man and God in the Flood and in the Babel story. We also notice worsening relations between man and animals after the Flood. God told Noah, "All wild animals and birds and fish will be afraid of you, for I have placed them in your power, and they are yours to use for food, in addition to grain and vegetables . . . and murder is forbidden. All man-killing animals must die, and the man who murders shall be killed; for to kill a man is to kill one made like God" (Gen. 9:2-6, *The Living Bible*). This passage indicates the anticipation of the growth of violence.

God's Cosmic Plan of Redemption and Reconciliation

No sooner was God's creation marred by sin than He

97

had a plan for its redemption. Before the foundation of the world He had made provision for this (Eph. 1:4). The redemption and the reconciliation are not for man alone, but for God's creation as well. God's covenant with Noah in Genesis 9 was not only with man, but with every living creature. Five times in this chapter He emphasizes that His covenant is with "every living creature" or "all flesh that is on the earth." We can see God's concern and His cosmic plan for all creation from Genesis 1 to Revelation 22. [1]

We have already noticed in chapter 4 that the reconciling of the world by Christ, like the Fall, was cosmic in effect. Not only was God in Christ reconciling man but also reconciling the world to Himself. Romans 8:18-25 teaches that God will deliver not only man but also His creature world. "The creature waits for the revelation of the sons of God." The redemption of the world depends upon man's redemption.

Thus we see that God was concerned not only in having a people but also a habitation for His people. His creation included animals, birds, fish, and creeping things. He created man to name and care for them. In God's sight these have value in themselves in addition to contributing to man's pleasure and wealth. The Christian steward therefore must be concerned about the welfare of the earth, its atmosphere, and its creatures.

Is There an Ecology Crisis?

According to one writer the word "ecology" was used the first time in the English language in 1873 about one hundred years ago. It is a much-used word today. Ecology is the study of the relationship of man to other living creatures and to his environment. The rapid growth in population and industrialization, with their resultant pollution of air, water, and earth, has set off the alarm in many quarters. Some tell us that massive starvation is just around the corner, that with the present rate of pollution life on this planet can survive but a few decades. And in the not-too-distant future, if the population explosion continues at the present rate, there will not be standing room on the earth for its population.

Is what we hear the voice of the prophets of doom? Or, are we truly facing this frightful prospect? There is no unanimity of opinion. Some are crying the alarm while others try to promote optimism.

God entrusted to man a good world with pure air and water, with fertile soil and beautiful forests, with great deposits of minerals and tremendous resources of energy. This was an ideal habitation for man. God did not intend that man exploit His world and rob future generations of their inheritance.

One of the saddest commentaries on the stewardship of past generations is the barren hills where once stood beautiful forests, the farm land robbed of its fertility, the great gullies resulting from erosion and poor farming. Our rivers and lakes have been polluted until fish can no longer live in them. The air has been so polluted that the health of thousands is impaired. Entire species of animals and birds have become extinct because of man's ruthlessness and greed for gain. What has happened and is happening to our environment is cause for concern, if not alarm. Let us notice what students of ecology are saying.

Air Pollution

We are told that over 140 million tons of pollutants are put into the air each year over the United States. Most large cities have serious problems of air pollution. Airline pilots maintain that a brown shroud of pollution can be seen around almost every major city of the United States from a distance of 70 miles. From a recent scientific analysis of New York City's atmosphere the conclusion was made that the average New Yorker takes each day into his lungs the equivalent of toxic materials of 38 cigarettes. Over half the pollution can be traced to automobiles. They emit 450 million pounds of carbon monoxide into the air every day. Every major city has dangerous concentrations of this deadly gas.

Pollution of the air is a problem not only in the United States; it is a world problem. In Tokyo thousands of residents have been hospitalized because of air pollution. Many will not venture outside when pollution is at its worst without gauze masks. Oxygen vendors are common where one can purchase some whiffs of fresh air for a quarter.

Water Pollution

"Our rivers are rapidly becoming running sewers. Already more than 20 of our major rivers are polluted to the point that fish and other water life are dying." [2] The author of the above statement goes on to say that most of our lakes are being threatened. Lakes that once afforded good fishing today are dying from pollution dumped into them. Thousands of tons of waste are being run into the lakes daily. Again, this is not only an American concern, but is worldwide. The Swiss were alarmed to find that lakes Geneva and Constance are rapidly becoming murky from pollutants from cities and industries being dumped into them. The Rhine is so toxic that multitudes of fish have died, and even eels have difficulty surviving. Scientists predict that the Sea of Galilee, where the disciples caught multitudes of fish, will be doomed in a decade unless steps are taken to stop the flow of pollutants into it. Even our oceans are dying and aquatic life has diminished by 40 percent in the past 20 years, we are told.

Insecticides and Herbicides

Part of the pollution of the air and waters is due to the use of herbicides and insecticides. DDT has been widely used. It spreads easily and lasts long. It is found everywhere on the face of the earth. If a farmer in Germany would use it on his farm, some of it would get to you. These herbicides flow down our streams, into rivers and lakes and threaten the extinction of birds, fish, and animals. The cahow bird, a little larger than a pigeon, breeding only on the small islands off Bermuda, is one species threatened with extinction. A man by the name of David Wingate is making an effort to save it, but says he is losing ground because the eggs are not hatching well. He took the embryo chick from an egg and dissected it. Its tissues were filled with DDT. It is a sea-feeding bird, and the fish are contaminated with DDT that gets into our waters.

The Department of the Interior lists 101 species of animals, birds, and fish that face extinction, many of which are threatened mainly because of pollutants, especially pesticides, or by destruction of their habitats. Certain birds that ingest pesticides lay thin-shelled eggs that never hatch. We are told that chemical pesticides have penetrated into the tissues of living animals and humans. "Most mothers' milk contains so much DDT that it would be declared illegal in interstate commerce if it were sold as cow's milk." [3]

Ruthless Slaughter of God's Creatures

Another sad commentary on man's stewardship is the ruthless way in which he has slaughtered the beasts of the field, the birds of the air, and the fish of the sea, some of them to extinction. In his love to possess and in his love to kill, man has plundered and exploited God's creation. We need only mention the passenger pigeon, the buffalo, the seal, the whale, and the beaver.

At the beginning of the eighteenth century it was estimated that there were five billion passenger pigeons. In 1810 a flock was seen that was estimated as one mile wide, 240 miles long, including perhaps two billion birds. They nested in the forest with sometimes as many as a hundred nests in one tree. Their meat was tasty and good. Shoots were organized and marketing became big business. They were shipped by carloads. One New York trader is said to have handled 18,000 birds daily. Farmers shot them for hog feed. The last nest observed in the wild was in 1894. The species became extinct when the last captive hen died in a Cincinnati zoo in 1914.

A similar story can be written about the buffalo. At the time President Jefferson signed the Louisiana Purchase it was estimated that there were perhaps from 50,000,000 to 100,000,000 buffalo north of the Rio Grande. In 1832 a traveler wrote, "As far as eye could see the country seemed absolutely blackened by innumerable herds." In the 1860s while the Union Pacific was being built buffalo meat was in demand. William F. Cody (Buffalo Bill) helped supply the meat. He is credited with killing 4,280 in 18 months. Often only the tongues and perhaps a choice part of the rump were taken. The carcass was left to rot.

Buffalo were also slaughtered for their hides. At Ft. Worth hides were stacked high in rows a quarter of mile long awaiting shipment. By 1883 only one herd of about 10,000 remained in North Dakota. A party of hunters set out in September to exterminate them. One thousand were killed the first day. By November the American buffalo had just about ceased to exist.[4]

Some authorities claim that the main purpose in the extermination of the buffalo was to deprive the Plains Indian of food. After the main source of his livelihood was removed the Indian was subdued and could be moved to the reservation.

The raid on wildlife included also the beaver and the seal. Groups were organized to go up the rivers trapping beavers. Trappers made a livelihood and organizers made a fortune as pelts were shipped to Europe by the hundreds of thousands. Raids were made on large herds of seals in the North Pacific until only 3 percent of the original population remained.

Stewards of the Soil

"And the Lord God placed the man in the Garden of Eden as its gardener, to tend and care for it" (Gen. 2:15, *The Living Bible*).

The Christian steward is aware that he does not own the land, "The earth is the Lord's." Man is the "gardener," not the owner. Upon a thin layer of topsoil the people of the world are dependent for their food. The fate of this and succeeding generations depends much upon how this thin layer is tilled and conserved. As stewards of God, as His gardeners, we are morally obligated to dress and keep the ground so that its fertility and productivity are passed on to succeeding generations.

There is a close relationship between soil conservation and soul conservation. In the areas of our nation where the land has been ruined by failure to apply conservation principles, where the soil has been depleted, local churches flounder on the brink of bankruptcy. There was a time when the slogan was, "Plow up, wear out, move on." The great dust storms of the thirties, the millions of wind-ruined acres ravaged by winds and by repeated floods, pointed up the selfishness of wasteful farming.

Man's violation of stewardship principles because of his greed for gain often has chain reactions. Overlogging and plundering the forests resulted in erosion and floods. Overgrazing the pastureland brought barrenness and deserts. Over-farming brought with it the dust storms of the thirties and serious erosion of the soil. Former Secretary of the Interior, Steward L. Udall, in *The Quiet Crisis* writes, "The settlers thus set the stage for the Dust Bowl of the 1930s — the most tragic land calamity ever to strike the North American continent.

"In the long run overgrazing and overfarming proved as disastrous as overmining and overlogging. Yet the raids on the resources were not limited to soil or gold or timber. They extended to biological resources as well. The big raid on wildlife began when the voyagers and colonists found that pelts would fetch a good price in European markets." [5]

It has been estimated that over 280 million acres of crops and grazing lands in the United States have been ruined or seriously damaged by erosion, and that 775 million acres more of crop, grazing, and forest lands have been affected.

One high school textbook stated that each year enough topsoil is removed from our American farms by wind and water to fill a freight train all the way to the moon and halfway back. In Arkansas there are acres of barren rock where once was good grazing land. When the cotton gin was invented farmers plowed up this grazing land and planted it to cotton for a quick profit. Rains washed the loose soil down the creeks until today there are just a few growing shrubs from crevices in the rock.

In the August 26, 1972, issue of the *Saturday Review* appeared an article on strip mining in West Virginia. In the steep terrain the coal seams are exposed by blasting away the whole mountainside. The slides bury fertile bottom lands and choke streams. The landscape is forever marred by serpentile scars, notched in once fertile slopes. The human cost in this process is also high. People are driven from their homes, or remain to witness the destruction of the surrounding countryside. Seven thousand strip miners displace several times that number of deep miners, who often are unsuited for other work. Some leaders, like John D. Rockefeller, Jr., are saying that strip mining is a social and economic disaster to the state.

A book like *The Quiet Crisis* by former Secretary of the Interior Udall makes one keenly aware of man's failure to observe stewardship principles in caring for God's creation. Man has exploited, plundered, and ravaged the generous supply of resources entrusted to him by God. This he has often done ignorantly and with no evil intentions. Much of it has been done in the name of progress. The forests, like the Indians, were an obstacle to settlement and farming, and had to be eradicated. The buffalo were a chief source of sustenance for the Indians and therefore had to be exterminated.

But perhaps nothing has contributed more to the exploitation of resources and to the pollution of our environment than two things that rate high in the priority of Americans — money and time. We dump pollutants into our streams and rivers because it is the cheapest and quickest way to get rid of them. We tear up and destroy our land by strip mining because it is the least expensive in money and time. Methods of conservation are more expensive and time-consuming, at least for the moment.

Reason for Optimism

The people who have been pointing out the dangerous and wasteful roads upon which we have been traveling have rendered us a real service. The fact that so many people are concerned about our "crisis" is encouraging. Forward steps in conservation are being taken. Laws are being passed and enforced. Industrialists, who have often contributed much to pollution, are taking steps not only to discontinue methods that make for pollution, but steps that will be remedial in effect.

Some industries take pride in their accomplishments in anti-pollution. Some believe that there is a real chance of anti-pollution becoming big business and quite lucrative. With all the furor about pollution it would be surprising if some enterprising persons do not try to commercialize anti-pollution. There is evidence that this is already being done.

In a late issue of *U.S. News and World Report* appears an encouraging article about industry stepping in to help save our environment. Lakes, hills, and forests are being donated by large companies so that preservation can be assured.

A New Jersey company turned over a Virginia swamp near the coast to be preserved rather than plowed up. It will be a refuge for wildlife near the streets of Norfolk. It is a tract of almost 50,000 acres worth 12.6 million dollars.

A multimillion dollar stretch of woodlands in Minnesota was donated by a power company. A hilly expanse bordering the Pacific in California was given by an oil company. An investment firm in New York donated a region of deep forest and lakes in Vermont in which smallmouth bass abound.

Many companies with large holdings are making areas

106

available to hikers, campers, and hunters. Some of these industrialists have had to resist severe pressure from real-estate agents and also from local governments interested in developing primitive areas. There is hope for environmental preservation when people begin to place it above profits.

While there are some who believe that in some areas we have crossed the line of no return, others are confident that we have what it takes to meet the situation head-on and win. Some economists are saying that the earth could never support its growing population, but there are others who disagree. While it is a mistake to think that the resources of our planet are limitless, we must realize they are tremendous.

"Harold G. Moulton, former president of the Brookings Institution, in one of the most significant studies of modern times, gives the highly documented result of thirty years of exhaustive research by the institution scientists. The conclusion is that there is no known limit to the potential wealth of the world. He declares that the natural resources and productive capacity of the United States alone could, in the year 2050, support a population of 300,000,000 at a standard of living eight times as high as that of today. He states that the basic raw materials for such an expansion are adequate for centuries to come. New techniques and chemicals will stretch existing supplies almost endlessly. The chemist and the agricultural scientist are proving in this respect to be partners of God. . . . The tillable area of the earth can easily be doubled and the natural endowments of the earth are adequate to support high standards of living for the earth's teeming millions for all time to come."

The author continues, "This study is supported by Charles E. Kellog, chief of Soil and Survey Division of the U.S. Department of Agriculture. 'Considering the new technology, I am confident food can be produced for twice the world's present population.' " [6]

Some ecology alarmists warn that the present rate of consumption of energy will deplete the resources of the world in a few decades. Others point out that God has supplied the universe with almost unlimited supplies of energy. As common sources of energy are used up, the God-given ingenuity of man will, no doubt, discover new sources of power. If the energy of the sun could be harnessed there would be no end of energy. The depths of the earth are bursting with power, waiting to be tapped.

We are told that today nearly a score of nations have begun to tap geo-thermal energy, earth-heat miles deep in the earth. A U.N. director of resources and transport is credited with saying, "I believe that we are witnessing the birth of a vast new source of energy." He told newsmen that this type of energy was making a breakthrough and was widespread, clean, and cheap.

Fifteen to twenty-five miles underground is molten rock, or magma; where there are fissures in the earth, it pushes closer to the surface. The molten rocks heat the underground water into hot reservoirs, six miles or less from the surface. Hot water and steam that can find their way out become hot springs or geysers. If not, wells drilled down can tap these reservoirs. The steam or hot water can be used to generate electric power.

In California geo-thermal energy is being used to generate power. While the amount generated at this time is not great, an Interior Department panel estimated last year that geo-thermal energy in the United States could, by the year 2000, supply 395 million kilowatts, more than all United States electric generating capacity today. It requires less capital investment to build a geo-thermal plant and takes only two years to build it. [7]

The Attitude of the Christian Toward His Environment

What then should be the attitude of the Christian toward the ecological debate? Always the Christian should approach problems such as this with faith and courage, avoiding the human tendency to become panicky. We should not be hasty to climb aboard bandwagons and should avoid being fadchasers. Someone has said that Americans tend to be a problem-a-year people. One year it is race, the next year woman's lib, then ecology. This may help bring issues to the forefront but contributes little to their solution. We may contribute to the noise but help little in lifting the burden. A few suggestions may be in order.

1. We need a proper theology of God, man, and creation.

God is infinite and sovereign. He therefore is unique and above man and other created creatures. He is Creator, Sustainer, and Redeemer. He is a personal God, yet present in His creation. In Christ He was reconciling the world to Himself.

Man is a finite being, like other of God's creatures. But man was created in God's image and can relate to God. While created as were other creatures, he is above them. But he should share the Creator's concern for all living creatures.

While God gave man dominion over the earth, he must never take this as a license to misuse and exploit the earth. Man's dominion is under the dominion of the Creator. As steward, man has a responsibility to God, to His creatures, and to His created world. He is God's agent in helping reconcile the world to God.

When God created the heavens and the earth, the vegetation, the animals, birds and fish, He declared them "good." They had value in themselves. As stated before, when man sinned the creation was subjected to "vain-

109

ness." It no longer filled the place God intended. But God's plan of redemption included all His creation, not only man. In commenting on Romans 8 Francis Shaeffer says, "What Paul says here is that when our bodies — bodies of men — are raised from the dead, at that same time nature, too, will be redeemed. The blood of the Lamb will redeem man and nature together, as it did in Egypt at the time óf the Passover, when the blood applied to the doorposts saved not only the sons of the Hebrews but also their animals." [8]

Too often Christian ethics and Christian theology have pretty well limited their discussions to man's relationship to God and to man. Omitting man's relation to God's creation is a serious omission. This inadequacy in theology and ethics, no doubt, has been partially responsible for man's arrogant attitude toward nature and the earth and for exploitation and pollution. On the other hand, we must avoid the other extreme, that of nature worship, denounced in no uncertain terms in the first chapter of Romans. We need to see nature not only as an object of creation but also as an object of redemption. It therefore is of real value to God. We are stewards in helping make nature what God wants it to be.

2. We should realize that in the stewardship of our earth, our decisions and actions have direct and indirect effects upon ourselves. "We do not forsake cleanliness without a loss of self-respect. We cannot turn our backs on beauty without losing cultural stature. We do not heedlessly exterminate the passenger pigeon or decimate the Great Plains Indian without some stain on our shield, without its effect on the national conscience and character. We are what we have done. But what we have created can destroy us." [9]

We exploit and abuse nature and its resources only at

great hurt to ourselves and to future generations. It is God's earth. We are His caretakers.

3. We must put stewardship of God's creation above financial gain. One major reason that ecological fervor died down so soon after Earth Day is that the American people found out that cleaning up the environment was going to cost them. We want pure water, pure air, and beautiful surroundings, but we have second thoughts about it if it means increased taxes, higher priced commodities, or cash out of pocket. If we are going to be good stewards of our environment we will have to give up the mania for the "quick buck." We must take a long-range view of things. In the long run we and our posterity will be far better off caring for and conserving natural resources and cleaning up the environment. We may not reap as large a harvest this year, but we will be making possible larger harvests and more pleasant surroundings in the future.

4. We must emphasize again nonconformity to the world and be ready to adopt new lifestyles. James M. Houston in writing on the environmental movement suggests, "The Christian must lead in a new lifestyle that encompasses all these needs. Where does he begin? Perhaps in the regular tithing of his income. Learning to give first a tenth and then even more of it will tell the world more about his responsible stewardship on behalf of the earth and his fellowmen than any academic discussion. This reduction in income can begin to count environmentally when he runs his car as long as the body and engine hold together and runs his house within simple economy. This is one way Christians can start to control the environmental crisis now upon us."[10]

H. Barnette in *The Church and the Ecological Crisis* tells us that 6 percent of the population of the world lives in the United States and consumes approximately 50 percent of the world's resources. Another writer says we are responsible for 50 percent of the pollution. Another estimates that the average white, middle-class American baby has a future consumption and pollution fifty times greater than a baby born in Calcutta. Mr. Burnette tells us that there is a systematic attempt on the part of the business community to encourage Americans to develop buying habits that turn consumers into wasteful, debt-ridden, and permanently discontented persons — all under the guise to "Keep America strong." They are encouraging the throw-away spirit in a throw-away society. "The markets are glutted with nonessential and inferior goods. To end this 'glut' the marketing experts encourage gluttony.[11]

> "The Christian style of life as portrayed in the New Testament is characterized by discipline: personal discipline and discipline in the family (Eph. 6:1-4), modesty in dress (1 Tim. 2:9; 1 Pet. 3:3), self-control and godliness (Tit. 2:12). A recovery of biblical style of life is essential not only because it is Christian, but also for the reason that it contributes to a healthy environment. If Christians persist in living by the standards of this world, they will have no distinctive lifestyle and no model of discipline in an undisciplined society."[12]

5. The voice of the church must be heard. The church if it is really concerned about the stewardship of the gospel must speak out on issues like war, racism, and ecology. The Bible has something to say on these issues, so must the church. Stewardship is as much a Christian doctrine as is justification or sanctification, and stewardship of the earth is a vital part of man's stewardship. The environmental issue is not only a practical issue; it also has religious and moral implications. It involves not only man's relation to nature, but also his relation to man and to God. When man depletes the soil, destroys the trees, exploits the natural

resoures, pollutes the air and water, and exterminates earth's creatures, he robs and impoverishes his fellowmen. He violates the stewardship laws of God.

The church cannot close its eyes to these sins. The church must help its members see that God is sovereign Owner of the earth and that His interests involve the best interests of man and of the world. Man must become a partner of God in promoting His benevolent purposes in the world. He must see that all creatures and all creation in the eyes of God have value in themselves. Man must be made conscious of his responsibility to God, his fellowmen, and creation.

6. Instead of seeking for earthly gain we should seek the gain that comes through "godliness with contentment." As Christians we should resist the tremendous pressures to engage and indulge in extravagant and needless consumerism, a primary source of pollution. People are pressured by commercials to buy what they want instead of what they need. They are urged to go on a "saving spree." The only limit to the amount they can "save" is the amount of savings they are willing to spend.

As a result of this consumerism we have boxes of slightly used clothing, discarded utensils, dishes, and furniture. Disposal of garbage, paper, and trash becomes a major problem in our cities and communities. Principles of conservation would help in the solution of this problem.

Nearly ten million cars will be discarded in 1973. Many of these, with a little expense, could serve adequately for another year or two. Recently the Highway Department of Kansas advertised a sale of a couple hundred cars, trucks, and trailers that had been abandoned along the highway and never claimed. These were picked up within a radius of around a hundred miles. What would the number be for the entire nation?

It becomes evident that in meeting the ecological crisis a radical change in lifestyles is essential. We must resist the tendency to extravagance and wastefulness and adopt principles of conservation. We must practice Christian self-denial and not let human wants dictate our mode of living.

A number of ways each of us could help implement point six are:

1. Set our minds on things that are above, not on things on the earth (Col. 3:2).

2. Cultivate the spirit of contentment encouraged by the Apostle Paul in 1 Timothy 6:6-11.

3. Seek to limit rather than expand individual wants. Spend for needs rather than wants.

4. Get maximum use from "things" instead of discarding them when slightly used.

5. Promote and cooperate in recycling paper, metals, glass, etc.

6. Avoid being a "litterbug." Form the habit of picking up gum and candy wrappers, empty cigarette packages, beer cans, etc., thrown away by careless litterbugs.

7. Plant a tree, a rosebush, or a flower garden. You may not be able to eat them, but their beauty will add to the beauty of the earth and to the beauty of your personality.

8. Provide food for birds and wild animals when natural supplies are limited.

9. Instead of burning leaves and grass, make compost piles that can return organic matter to the soil, and avoid more air pollution.

10. In going short distances walk, ride a bicycle, run, or jog. It will put you and the environment in better condition.

11. If possible, cut down on your driving. Use mass

transportation or car pools when possible. Automobiles produce 60 percent of the nation's air pollution.

12. Shut off the motor when parked. The worst pollution occurs when the motor is idling.

13. Conserve heat and electricity. They put smog in the air and pollution in the rivers. Do not overheat homes and offices, and turn off lights when not in use.

These are but a few suggestions. You can think of many more ways to help to control the environment. The number of small ways in which one can contribute are almost limitless.

To do some of these things may take a bit more time and put no cash in our pockets, but they will contribute to greater values. The contribution by one individual may seem small and insignificant, but if practiced by two hundred million people the results would be tremendous.

8

STEWARDSHIP OF THE GOSPEL

"A stewardship of the gospel is committed to me" (1 Cor. 9:17).

A number of years ago a minister of the gospel accepted a pastorate where the members were giving about $7,000 annually for missions but had a much larger local budget. This pastor was deeply concerned for his congregation and especially for the stewardship of the gospel. He knew that in many homes in his parish there was temporal prosperity, but no joy and Christian victory. There were other homes where joy was deep and genuine.

This pastor knew that the difference lay in commitment and in the stewardship of giving. He preached spiritual messages. He set up a year-round stewardship emphasis and implemented a friendly visitation program — the Every Member Canvass. He urged that at least 50 percent of the church's giving go for missions. The results were astounding. In three years the church was giving for missions around $30,000, an increase of over 300 percent! Imagine what that did for stewardship of the gospel!

But many by-products will result in a situation like this one. The giving for the local budget also increased.

People found new joy in their lives. One member declared, "I used to give little and it hurt. Now I give a lot and it is the best pleasure I have in life." As a result of this church's performance, other churches followed the example and increased their giving. The spiritual life became also more vital. The pastor stated that several years' experience justified accepting the New Testament promises concerning Christian stewardship which they should have accepted by faith. He declared also that stewardship must be spiritually motivated and must be stewardship of the gospel.

This pastor is a good example of a true steward of the gospel. He promoted the spiritual life of God's people and the support of the kingdom of God. He set an example for other churches to follow. The results were worldwide. What it would mean to the spiritual life of our churches and to the stewardship of the gospel if pastors everywhere would follow this pastor's example!

Stewardship of the Gospel Promotes God's Purposes

Many people have a very narrow conception of stewardship of the gospel. They seem to think that it means merely taking the gospel to the world and making disciples. This, of course, is an important part, but to the Apostle Paul stewardship of the gospel meant far more than that. He would have felt delinquent in thus limiting the gospel. Stewardship of the gospel means promoting God's eternal purposes.

We are also mistaken when we think that God had one purpose in the Old Testament and another in the New Testament. As noticed before, God's purposes are eternal, but progression occurs in their fulfillment. When God's purposes for His people are fully realized in the new heaven and the new earth, they will be what He purposed before the worlds were formed. "My counsel shall stand, and I will do all my pleasure. . . . Yea, I have spoken it, I will also bring it to pass" (Is. 46:10, 11).

What Stewardship of the Gospel Meant to Paul

Paul was conscious that he was a steward of the gospel. "Let a man so account of us, as of the ministers of Christ, and stewards of the mysteries of God" (1 Cor. 4:1). In his letter to the Ephesians he states that a stewardship of the grace of God is given him. Because of this keen sense of stewardship he labored night and day. He determined to know nothing but Jesus and Him crucified. As much as was in him, he was determined to preach the gospel. He declared intensely, "Woe is unto me, if I preach not the gospel."

The apostle to the Gentiles was deeply concerned in preaching the gospel and in winning men to Christ. He declared that he had become all things to all men that he might by all means save some. But Paul saw stewardship of the gospel as something far greater than merely preaching and winning men to Christ. He was interested also in establishing churches, communities of God. He was interested in developing converts to Christianity to spiritual maturity and in perfecting them for the work of the ministry. Stewardship of the gospel meant leading people to unity of the faith, with men becoming perfect men and growing into the stature of Christ.

Paul was also deeply concerned in meeting the physical needs of people. When people for whom Christ died, and in whom He dwelt, were in bodily need Paul could not be indifferent to those needs. He saw stewardship of the gospel not only as redemption of the souls of men but also as the redemption of the physical, social, moral, and economic areas of life — not only winning people to the

118

community of God, but helping them be the kind of people He wants in His community.

Stewardship of the Gospel as Seen in Romans

The above facts become evident in reading any of Paul's epistles. Perhaps the Book of Romans points out as clearly as any what stewardship of the gospel meant to Paul. He refers to his message in Romans as, "my gospel" (2:16). What does his gospel include?

1. In the first two and one half chapters he points to man's need, his lostness. "When they knew God, they glorified him not as God . . . their foolish heart was darkened . . . they did not like to retain God in their knowledge, God gave them over to a reprobate mind." Because of this the wrath of God is revealed from heaven. Man is inexcusable and will be judged. Not only are all men sinful, but all of man is sinful and by the deeds of the law no flesh can be justified. Man is hopelessly lost and there is nothing he can do about it. This truth is a part of the gospel.

2. In the next two and one half chapters Paul tells us God has provided a new way for man to be righteous before God, "But now the righteousness of God without the law is manifested." By the grace of God, through Christ's blood, and by faith of Christ, there is "remission of sins that are past, through the forbearance of God." Now man may be justified by faith without the deeds of the law. Because we are justified by faith, we have peace with God, we rejoice in hope of God's glory, and we have the love of God shed abroad in our hearts. This is the gospel.

3. In the next three chapters (6, 7, 8) Paul tells us how we may live the life God wants us to live. It is one thing to be saved; it is another thing to live the Christian life. Just as salvation is by faith, so we live the Christ

119

life by faith. The Galatians were saved by faith, then turned to the deeds of the flesh for living the Christian life. Paul calls them "foolish Galatians." Too many Christians do the same. They accept Christ by faith, then say, "Now I must quit doing this; I must do that," only to experience Romans 7.

Paul shows us that the Christian life is lived by faith. We are to know that we have been crucified with Christ. We are to reckon ourselves dead. We are not to yield the members of our bodies to sin, but yield them to God. We are to walk not after the flesh but after the Spirit. All this means faith, dependence upon God's Spirit.

This is vividly brought out as we compare Romans 7 and 8. If in the King James version you count the number of times "I" is mentioned in the seventh chapter you will count 33. Not once will you find Spirit (with capital S). No wonder he cries out:

> "I do not understand my own actions. For I do not do what I want, but I do the very thing I hate. . . . For I do not do the good I want, but the evil I do not want is what I do. . . . Wretched man that I am! Who will deliver me from this body of death?" (7:15-24, RSV).

On the contrary, in Romans 8 "I" appears only twice and Spirit 19 times! Paul can conclude this chapter, "Nay, in all these things we are more than conquerors through him that loved us." When we walk after the Spirit and not after the flesh, the law of the Spirit of life in Christ Jesus makes us free from the law of sin and death.

To help people see and realize these great truths and to help them to a Christlike walk are a definite part of the stewardship of the gospel. The true steward of the gospel will never be satisfied with merely a first commitment to Christ.

4. Paul then in the next three chapters (9, 10, 11) shows his deep concern and heavy burden for his misguided brethren, the Jews who are separated from Christ. He speaks of their past, present, and future and uses them to illustrate the doctrine of justification by faith. Israel is not lost because God turned His back on the Jews and now accepts Gentiles. Repeatedly he says there is no difference between Jew and Gentile. "If thou shalt confess with thy mouth the Lord Jesus, and shalt believe in thine heart that God raised him from the dead, thou shalt be saved." This applies to Jew and Gentile alike.

Israel is lost because "being ignorant of God's righteousness, and going about to establish their own righteousness, [they] have not submitted themselves unto the righteousness of God." They were cut off because of unbelief. The Gentiles were grafted in because of faith. Gentiles must take heed lest they be cut off because of unbelief. But if Israel believes they will be grafted in.

5. In the largest section of Romans, from the twelfth chapter to the end, Paul tries to show the Roman Christians what fruit a justified and sanctified life should yield. He points out the kind of community God wants His people to be. This is a most important part of stewardship of the gospel. We are not genuine stewards of God if we are not trying to shape our lives according to God's will, if we are not conforming to the image of His Son, and if we are not helping to shape the kind of community God desires.

Stewardship of the gospel is concerned not only in proclaiming correct doctrine. It is equally concerned that doctrine expresses itself in practical Christian living. Chapter 12 of Romans is one of the greatest stewardship passages in the entire Bible. It has to do with the stewardship of all of life, which is what the stewardship of the gospel is all about.

That stewardship of life was important to Paul and his gospel is underscored in the first verse of chapter 12: "I beseech you therefore" — "I plead with you." Why the "therefore"? Because of all the doctrinal truths he has given in the first eleven chapters. You are now justified by faith. You have been crucified with Christ and raised in newness of life. The law of the Spirit now makes you free from the law of sin and death. You have peace with God, and the love of God is shed abroad in your hearts — "therefore" they were to show it by grateful sacrifice, by new lifestyles, by faithful membership in the body of Christ, by using their gifts for the good of the body, by showing love and honor to the brotherhood, by generous giving for the needy, by a life of joy and patience, by accepting others and identifying with their joys and sorrows, by a life of nonresistance and peace, and by ministering to the needs of enemies.

God wants to see these Christlike qualities in His community of love and righteousness. Since the fall of man God has been striving to develop these traits in His people. For millennia God has been pleading, disciplining, chastising, and teaching His people to prepare them to be such persons. The prophets were His stewards in rebuking and exhorting Israel that they might conform to His standards.

Like Paul we must be deeply concerned about this aspect of stewardship of the gospel. The mission of the church is not only to win men to Christ but also to bring saints to maturity in Christ. The steward must participate with Christ in removing walls of separation, walls that divide man from man, race from race, and man from God.

It seems natural for humans to build barriers. The Christian church has been guilty of this practice. We build national, racial, color, social, and ideological barriers. These barriers separate brother from brother, son of God from son of God. The steward must be partner with Christ in breaking down these walls of separation.

The new people of God are one — a community of dissimilar men, even former foes. In this community of God are no American, Chinese, or Indians; no black, brown, or white; no communist or anti-communist. As someone has stated, "National churches, race churches, class churches are false churches and already heretical."

The church must challenge its members and help them grow in the graces of Christ. It must help them be good stewards of abilities and talents. It must help them become a sharing community, giving generously to the needs of the community and to the world.

Paul saw the gospel as the power of God unto salvation. This salvation meant deliverance from the guilt and punishment of sin. It meant deliverance from the power of sin and from a life of defeat. It was the power to live a transformed life. It meant power to faithfully serve as a member of Christ's body. It meant accepting the weaker brother and helping bear his burden. It was enabling power to walk after the Spirit and not after the flesh.

As a steward of God, Paul prayed, preached, and labored that people everywhere might accept and experience the power of the gospel.

The New Birth Not an End in Itself

Paul realized that the new birth was not an end in itself, but the means to an end. The new birth is but the beginning of our transformation into the image of Christ from glory to glory. It is the beginning of a life of service to God and man. Stewardship of the gospel that does not promote growth in Christ, service to God, and ministering to one's fellowmen is not a full gospel.

In chapter 12 Paul emphasizes commitment to the

service of God and ministering to the body of Christ. In chapter 13 he deals with service in relation to government. Chapters 14 and 15 instruct us not to be judgmental toward those who differ with us. We should act charitably toward them, receiving them and following after the things that make for peace and that edify.

That Paul believed in this larger concept of stewardship of the gospel is indicated in his conclusion in chapter 15. He states that he has written of these things boldly as a minister of Jesus Christ to the Gentiles, "ministering the gospel of God." Seemingly Paul believed he had been a good steward of the gospel, "I have fully preached the gospel of Christ" (15:19).

Paul knew that it was not God's will that any should perish. Therefore he became all things to all men that he might by all means save some. But Paul also knew, as he wrote to the Christians at Thessalonica, that "this is the will of God, even your sanctification." The will of God is that people be saved, but it is equally His will that Christians conform to the image of Christ. This also became Paul's deep concern.

Paul told the Ephesian elders, "By the space of three years I ceased not to warn every one night and day with tears." He not only rejoiced in their salvation; he labored in anguish for their sanctification. This was as much a part of stewardship of the gospel as bringing them to a knowledge of salvation.

Paul's Motivation

What motivated Paul to give himself in stewardship of the gospel? He gives us a number of reasons in 2 Corinthians 5. First, "We must all appear before the judgment seat of Christ; that every one may receive the things done in his body, according to that he hath done, whether it be good or bad." Paul wanted to be sure that he could give a good account of what he had done in life. He also wanted other men to be ready to stand before God. "Knowing therefore the judgment of God we persuade men."

Second, "For the love of Christ constraineth us." If Christ was willing to die for the sins of the world, he too should be willing to spend and be spent to promote the glorious gospel. He should be ready to suffer shipwreck, persecution, and death.

Third, "Therefore, if any one is in Christ, he is a new creation." Paul was eager to preach the gospel because of what it could do for man and because of what man could become in Christ. He had seen many men who had been pagans but now were saints in Christ. He was eager to go to Rome and to Spain and other parts of the world to help men become what God wanted them to be.

Fourth, "God was in Christ, reconciling the world unto himself . . . and hath committed unto us the word of reconciliation. . . . We are ambassadors for Christ, as though God did beseech you by us: we pray you in Christ's stead, be ye reconciled to God." No one can experience in his own life the transforming power of Christ and realize the great purposes of God in reconciling the world to Himself without committing himself to the stewardship of the gospel.

These four great incentives should challenge and inspire every Christian to faithful stewardship of the gospel, to dedication of life and all his resources to the promotion of the gospel of the kingdom.

9

PAUL'S TEACHINGS
ON GIVING

The Apostle Paul had a burning conviction that he was a chosen vessel of God to take the gospel to the Gentiles. He was keenly aware that to him was committed a stewardship of the gospel. Paul's concept of stewardship of the gospel was broad enough and scriptural enough to give him a deep compassion for people in bodily need. He saw ministering to the needs of God's people as a vital part of stewardship of the gospel. In meeting physical needs Paul was promoting the purposes of God. He interrupted a fruitful ministry at Antioch to carry relief money to the needy Christians in Judea (Acts 11:27-30).

Seeing the suffering and need at Jerusalem and experiencing the blessings of sharing and helping meet that need, Paul felt the responsibility under God to arouse the churches to generous giving. He gave orders to the churches of Galatia and Corinth to follow the example of the church at Antioch and give for the needs of their brethren (1 Cor. 16:1, 2).

In writing his first letter to the believers at Corinth, Paul insisted on the unity of the local church as a fellowship of believers in Christ. He spoke of love as the great-

126

est quality of the Christian believer. He told them of the Lord's victory over death and that God gives us victory through the Lord Jesus. He exhorted them to be steadfast, unmovable, always abounding in the work of the Lord.

From the truth of the glorious resurrection and the blessed victory in Christ, he referred immediately to the "collection." He asked them to translate doctrine into life. He wanted them to apply his teachings to the life and need of the larger Christian community. In referring to 1 Corinthians 16:1, 2 the commentator, Lenski, remarks, " 'So also do ye,' a simple evangelical method is thus put into operation in all the churches under Paul's leadership — one good method and that for all. This is a good example for churches today."

When Paul saw need on one hand, and Christians with means on the other hand, stewardship of the gospel demanded that he use his influence to get needs and money together.

A year later Paul wrote his second letter to the church at Corinth. A year before they had expressed a willingness to give. Paul now urges them to make good their promise. In the eighth and ninth chapters of 2 Corinthians we have Paul's longest treatise on giving. In this passage we glean some fundamental concepts in the theology of stewardship, as well as timely suggestions for implementing a financial plan and program. Paul used some practical fund-raising techniques.

Paul Actively Solicited Funds and Promoted the Offering

The church need never apologize for doing the same. In fact, we are negligent in duty if we do not. Where there is real need on the one hand, and in the church those with resources who could meet the need, we should help get need and resources together.

With the plight of Pakistani, Vietnamese, and Arab refugees today, and of poverty-stricken people in America and in other parts of the world, Christian churches would be less than "Christian" if they were not concerned and if they did not challenge their people to respond to these needs. We ought to do this not only because the poor people need help, but also because people with wealth need to share and give. Perhaps the greatest need is the latter one. It seems Paul felt this way.

It is doubtful whether the brethren in Judea received a greater blessing from the gift from Antioch than the givers themselves experienced. Paul and his helpers also greatly benefited by extracting the gift and administering it. Best of all, it brought glory and praise to God.

The collections for the saints would never have been given if Paul had waited for the churches to become spiritually mature. He was helping them become spiritually mature by challenging them to compassionate sharing and giving, by promoting Christian stewardship. The needs of the church were met because a man of God saw the need, adopted a practical financial plan, and had the courage to solicit from those who were capable of giving from that which they had.

Paul challenged the Corinthians by the liberality of the Macedonians. He had also challenged the Macedonians by the readiness of the Corinthians to give. This was effective. Paul tells the Corinthians that he had boasted to the Macedonians about their willingness to give and remarks, "Your enthusiasm has stirred most of them to give" (2 Cor. 9:2, Laubach). No doubt his reference to the liberality of the Macedonians also stirred the Corinthians to give.

Paul did not hesitate to use tact, or "psychology." In doing so he was merely using good common sense, and was using it for the glory of God. By using Paul's techniques many pastors could double the giving of their congregations. It might be that this would be the most effective stewardship of the gospel in which they had ever engaged. It would add to the spiritual maturity of the members as well as add significantly to the outreach of the church.

Paul Did Not See Giving as a By-Product of Grace

Every pastor should be aware of this truth, and he should have a real concern that his members "abound in this grace also." Paul often refers to giving as a grace of God. He reminds them of the example of our Lord, "For ye know the grace of our Lord Jesus Christ, that, though he was rich, yet for your sakes he became poor, that ye through his poverty might be rich" (2 Cor. 8:9).

The desire to give is a grace from God. The practice of giving will help us abound in this grace. Not only does grace cause us to give, but giving also promotes the grace. Just as faith is strengthened by the exercise of faith and the power to live an overcoming life is strengthened by living the overcoming life, so the grace of giving blossoms as one gives. True, these are gifts of God, but not apart from one's appropriating them by faith in action.

Paul shows that giving is to the glory of God. "The reason we are collecting this aid for the Christians at Jerusalem is because it brings glory to God. It also shows that the people of God are willing to help each other" (2 Cor. 8:19, Laubach).

How this lofty concept of Christian stewardship needs to be promoted in our churches today! How tragic when the church budget, the Every Member Enlistment, solicitation of funds, the offering, and the financing of the work of the kingdom is considered a mundane thing — as something almost unworthy of the Christian church. The promotion of the "collection" as we have it in the eighth and ninth chapters of 2 Corinthians is stewardship of the gospel on a high plane.

Money in the hands of a profligate may be "filthy lucre," but the money Paul solicited and administered for the saints never soiled his hands. It was a glory to God, a blessing to the givers, a witness to the world, a cause of praise to God from the beneficiaries, and a credit to the great apostle to the Gentiles.

Paul Saw Giving as Both Effect and Cause

Their rededication — first giving themselves to the Lord — no doubt influenced the Macedonians in their decision to give. The test of their dedication, however, was shown by giving. Paul was not deceived by that half truth, believed by many, "Get a man's heart right and he will give." How will a man's heart ever be right with God if it is filled·with covetousness and greed? The hearts of many are not right because of wrong attitudes toward money.

The heart condition does affect one's attitude toward wealth, but one's attitude toward riches also affects the condition of his heart. Jesus said, "Where your treasure is, there will your heart be also." He did not say if your heart is right the treasure will be at the right place. He did not begin working in an abstract way on the heart. He said, "Lay up for yourselves treasures in heaven."

Jesus did not tell the rich young ruler, "Get your heart right and you will share your riches." He told him if he wanted to be perfect he should get money matters straight, sell and give to the poor and he will have treasures in heaven. Likewise, when Zacchaeus told Jesus that he was giving half his goods to the poor and restoring fourfold any ill-gotten gain, Jesus answered, "Today salvation has come to this house." Getting the money question right helped get the heart right. The act of giving did not bring salvation. His decision to do this, however, contributed to and evidenced saving faith. If wrong attitudes toward money can drown men in perdition, surely changing those attitudes can bring salvation, if the attitude toward money is what it is that stands in the way.

Any minister who takes the attitude, "Get the heart right and giving will take care of itself," will be an ineffective pastor and will do gross injustice to his people. Unless people are taught and challenged to give and share they will not grow spiritually as they should. There is little that a pastor can do that will bring greater joy and blessing to his people than to develop in them the spirit of generous giving.

Giving generously to missions will increase one's interest in missions. Bringing the tithes and offerings to the church will increase one's love for and interest in the church and the kingdom. We are inclined to say, "Get them interested and they will give." True, but it's also true that giving increases interest. Here again cause and effect is a two-way street.

Byfield and Shaw in their book, *Your Money and Your Church,* say that any church that honestly and fearlessly approaches the problem of stewardship will not be disappointed in the results. "Attendance will increase; a new interest in study groups and adult classes will be seen; church-school teachers and church workers will appear from almost nowhere; the life of the church will take on a whole new tone in the congregation; and, just incidently, most churches will find that they have solved their money problems completely and painlessly." [1]

Paul Taught Proportionate Giving

"If a man is willing to give what he can, God accepts that. God judges a man's giving by what he has, and does not expect him to give if he is not able. I do not mean to let other churches off easily while you carry the burden. No, I mean that every person should give according to his ability to give. You are prospering now while the churches of Macedonia are in want. So you are able to supply what they could not give. Some other time they may have plenty and you may have need of help. Then they will be able to supply what you lack. Thus you will help one another" (2 Cor. 8:12-14, Laubach).

Paul had witnessed the church at Antioch give as each one was able for the brethren at Jerusalem. He with Barnabas delivered the gift. He ordered the churches of Galatia and the church at Corinth to give regularly as God prospered them. The area of finance in man's life is hardly exempt from the principle, "Freely ye have received, freely give."

We notice also this principle of proportionate giving, or giving according to ability, in Acts 11:29 and 1 Corinthians 16:1, 2. This principle of giving is found not only in the New Testament, but has its roots in the Old Testament (Deut. 16:10, 17), and seems to be related to if not identical with the law of the tithe. Here Israel is instructed to give as they are able, "according as the Lord thy God hath blessed thee." This was in connection with the festivals at Jerusalem. Israel was instructed to set aside the tithes of their income for these festivals. [2] It would appear, therefore, that giving according to the blessing of the Lord, or according to ability, may have been synonymous with the rendering of tithes.

Giving proportionately of one's income would certainly have the sanction of both Testaments. What proportion should be given is not specifically stated by Paul. It may have been the tithe, and most certainly would not have been less than that. Many people today find the tithe a satisfactory measure of proportionate giving. Others feel quite strongly that in an affluent society like ours, and with the needs of the world facing us, the tithe is too little. One brother declares that our churches today could give on the average 20 percent and should do so. With the vast amounts being spent for luxuries and pleasures by Christian people, it would be difficult to justify giving less than a tithe for the promotion of the Lord's work. Priorities would indeed have to be grossly distorted to defend giving any less.

Paul Stressed the Blessedness of Giving

Paul said to the Philippians, "I hold you in my heart" (1:7). Our churches today greatly need pastors like Paul, with a deep concern for their people. He was concerned in the Corinthian church and knew what it would mean to them if they did not fulfill their pledge and if they shut up their heart of compassion against the poor at Jerusalem. He knew the blessing that generous giving would bring them. Paul told the Ephesian elders that the Lord had said, "It is more blessed to give than to receive." Paul evidently believed this, and wanted his people to experience that blessedness.

Any pastor with a real love for his people will be concerned when his people do not respond to the grace of God and to the needs of His kingdom. If they are not sharing and giving generously, as God prospers, they are not in good spiritual health. They are missing out on the joy and the blessings God longs to give them. They need help. Paul felt that way about the saints at Corinth.

Paul told the Corinthians, "When Titus visited you

the other time he began to gather your gifts for the people of God in Jerusalem. . . . So we urged him to finish gathering these gifts of loving kindness" (2 Cor. 8:6, Laubach). Then in verse 16 he writes, "I thank God for putting in the heart of Titus so much loving concern for you." In soliciting funds Titus was doing so because of the loving concern he had for the Christians he was soliciting.

Solicitation of funds, the financial program of the church, should never lose sight of this stewardship truth. When Jesus told the rich young ruler to sell and give to the poor, His thoughts were not primarily with the poor. His love and concern was for the young man. God's purpose in the tithe was not for the sake of the tithe but for the sake of His people. The wise pastor will endeavor to lead his people to give liberally because of the blessing and the new life they will experience through it. Many are the testimonies I have heard such as, "How we have been blessed since we began tithing." One person thanked me for leading her and her family to see and experience the joy of tithing. She said, "I am now giving two tenths."

The needs of our colleges some years ago that practically forced solicitors on the field have resulted in far more than raising thousands of dollars for Christian education. The contribution this has made to increased giving, to the stewardship program of the church, and to the spiritual life of the church has, I believe, outweighed the dollar and cents value (and it may not always have been done with a loving concern for the giver). It seems to me this solicitation was necessary because of our stewardship immaturity. When, and if, we arrive at stewardship maturity, it should not be necessary to support a corps of solicitors to secure funds for the Lord's work.

134

Paul Was Careful in the Administration of the Funds

"We are careful and honest in managing these gifts of love, and we do not want even one person to doubt it. We want to do right, not only in God's sight, but also in the sight of all men" (2 Cor. 8:20, 21, Laubach). To make sure no suspicion will be aroused, Paul sends a third person along with their gifts, a person in whom they have confidence. Holmes Rolston has well said, "The springs of giving are certain to dry up when men begin to be doubtful about the way in which their money is being used."

Those responsible for handling and administering "gifts of love" contributed by loyal followers of Christ should consider it a sacred trust. They should see that these funds are rightly used and should exercise every care to avoid suspicion. The ones chosen to handle the offering should be trustworthy persons. To have two or more persons responsible for counting the offering before it is handed to the treasurer is a good practice. This does not necessarily mean that we do not trust the treasurer, but we want to save him from the chance of suspicion. One person should not be left alone with the offering until it has been counted and recorded.

This may seem to be overcautious, or lacking trust, but there are numerous cases where, under such circumstances, a person was tempted and did take money from the offering. One church leader reported a few years ago that this was going on in his church over a period of years. No one knows how much, but hundreds of dollars disappeared. I have heard of others who became conscience-smitten and confessed having pilfered funds. Every precaution should be taken to avoid this. Anyone soliciting funds should promptly issue receipts for a contribution and have a duplicate for himself. The books of every treasurer should be carefully audited. Again, these precautions are taken not so much because we distrust people but to protect them from temptation and suspicion.

A word of caution should be given here also to institutions of the church who have the responsibility of dispensing the tithes and offerings of their people. Every care should be taken to use wisely these contributions and to use them consistently with the wish of the donors. Reports on how the money was used should be available. Whenever people lose confidence in those who are dispensing their contributions, the inflow of funds will diminish or be directed through other channels. "It is required in stewards, that a man be found faithful."

Paul Insisted That the Offering Be Voluntary

After Paul had quoted the saying, "He who sows little will gather a little harvest; he who sows much will gather a big harvest," he says, "That is true. Yet each person must make up his own mind what he will give. He must not be pushed or compelled to give. God loves the man who is happy when he gives" (1 Cor. 9:6, 7, Laubach). In the stewardship program of the church there is no place for high-pressure methods. To some it might appear that Paul was high-pressuring the Corinthians. He was not. He did a good job of showing them their privilege in Christ, their responsibility to their brethren, and their Christian duty, but he let them decide what they were going to give.

A solicitor was once introduced as the biggest beggar in the world. He responded, "I'm not a beggar. I never begged for a dollar in my life. But I have given my friends some marvelous opportunities." Paul was giving the Christians some marvelous opportunities, but let each of them decide how to accept the challenge.

The stewardship program of the church must never

be built upon legalism or coercion. In soliciting funds for Christian purposes we should be interested in building character. We cannot build character by coercion. Every member, however, should be faced with his Christian responsibility toward his church and his fellowmen. Any Christian who has the means and does not support his church and the needs of the world is a sick person and needs help. It is not fair to members of the church to allow them to miss the joy and satisfaction of sharing in the support of their church and helping meet the needs of others.

Pastors and mature Christians should challenge and help others to grow and abound in this Christian grace. This is what stewardship is about. "Every man according as he purposeth in his heart, so let him give." It is not our duty to tell one how much to give, but it is our privilege in Christ to help him to higher and nobler purposes, to stimulate his purposes to give. That is what Paul was doing in 2 Corinthians 8 and 9.

Paul Tried to Remove Fear and Inspire Faith

The tempter so often comes to Christians and whispers, "You cannot afford to tithe. If you do you will not be able to meet your bills. You must provide for your own; you cannot make that mission pledge." Paul knew how subtle the suggestions of the enemy could be. He told the Corinthians, "But do not let fear for the future prevent you from being generous. God is able to bless you with more than you need. He will give you so much that you will always be able to give to every good cause." If pastors today assured and challenged their members as Paul did, it would mean much in their stewardship and in their joyful experience in Christ.

Giving is often a test of faith. People just do not believe it is more blessed to give than to receive. They do not believe the promises of God for generous giving. They somehow cannot grasp the truth that if they sow bountifully they will reap bountifully.

When we believe God is asking us to give generously for a cause, we need not ask, "But how will we meet our bills?" Many have had the joyous experience of being deeply moved because of some pressing need and of giving the last dollar when they themselves had needs. Invariably, they found that giving that last dollar did not hurt them but rather brought blessing. One cannot outdo God when it comes to giving. We need not let the fear of the future keep us from giving generously.

Paul Did Not Take an "Either/or" Attitude

Life in the Spirit in no sense means the denial of life in the body. To the Christian material things become sanctified for the purposes of God. The physical body becomes a living sacrifice presented to God, a holy temple of God. Money dedicated to God becomes a sacrifice, well-pleasing. It becomes a means of fellowshiping with the saints and of fellowship in the furtherance of the gospel. Jesus' testimony to John was, "The blind recover their sight, the lame walk, the lepers are made clean, the deaf hear, the dead are raised to life" (Lk. 7:22, NEB). The kingdom was spiritual but it was proclaimed by deeds done to weak, mortal bodies.

The Good Samaritan pouring oil on the wounds of the wounded man, the widow giving her two mites, the parable of the unjust steward, and the parable of the pounds all point to the importance Jesus attached to the material. The attitude of a person toward money and material treasure helps determine his fitness to administer spiritual things.

Paul saw clearly the relationship between the material and the spiritual and their interaction upon each other. He saw financial commitment as a part of total commitment to the gospel of Jesus Christ. As stated before, lack of funds in church treasuries is a symptom of unsound theology and inadequate moral commitment.

The matter of financial commitment should be a matter of concern to the Christian minister who is truly concerned for his people and in stewardship of the gospel. If he is not concerned here, just where are his interests? Is he concerned in the moral life of his people? Does church membership or attendance at the services of the church concern him?

Christian giving, as well as morality and church membership, is an important aspect of the total Christian life. A life of discipleship is not possible without it, and surely the pastor will be concerned for the discipleship of his people.

"Your giving will prove that your religion is real. If you make a generous gift to them and to others, every one will thank God and say: 'These Christians not only believe in Christ; they also practice what they believe' " (2 Cor. 9:13, Laubach).

Stewardship of the Gospel Must Include Possessions

Jesus saw money as His chief contender for the affections of man. When we realize that covetousness and materialism are evil cancers that can destroy man in perdition, and that the love of money is a root of all kinds of evil, we can see why emphasis on the stewardship of money is very important.

This conviction deepens when we realize, on the other hand, the tremendous power for good that lies in the right use of money. Yet, some object and ask, "Why talk about money? Preach the gospel." This sounds good but is neither scriptural nor logical. Generous giving and sharing are an important part of the gospel. How can we get people right with God when they are covetous or greedy?

An unwillingness on the part of Christians to share and give generously of what God has given them becomes a chief obstacle to stewardship of the gospel today. Better stewardship of the gospel is waiting for God's people to become so committed to Christ that they willingly and generously share the wealth that God has given them.

What will a pastor who is a good steward do? Does he merely preach, pray, and minister to spiritual needs of people? In a lost, sick, and needy world how does stewardship of the gospel manifest itself?

Let us suppose that a pastor has a church of 200 members. In the congregation are many with affluence and wealth, average income Americans. They spend large amounts of money upon themselves, but give less than half of the tithe to the church and to charitable causes. They give annually $35,000, but a mere tithe would be $100,000. The mission board and church institutions are badly in need of funds for stewardship of the gospel. Poverty areas are crying for help, millions are starving.

A situation like this should greatly concern a true steward of the gospel. The tithe from his people (and surely no Christian could justify giving less than a tithe in times like these and in face of world needs) would mean $65,000 more for the spread of the gospel and for feeding the hungry. This could mean a few more missionaries on the field and hundreds more people hearing the gospel. It could mean scores of lives saved. It would mean great blessing and new spiritual life to his people. It would mean treasures laid up in heaven.

One of the greatest contributions this pastor, and hundreds more like him, could make to the stewardship of the gospel would be to double or triple the giving in his church. This would do more for the stewardship of the gospel than all the eloquent sermons he might preach in a lifetime. It would add to the effectiveness of his pastoral ministry.

"Stewards of the gospel" is a great Christian concept. It can, however, become a cloak for selfishness, injustice, and neglect of duty. It can serve the purpose of self-justification for miserly giving and for lack of stewardship of possessions. Requests for funds can be shrugged off with, "We are stewards of the gospel." It can be a cover-up for shirking one's duties toward the oppressed, the underprivileged, and the needy. Efforts to minister relief and service to the needy and downtrodden may be discounted by the remark, "The Christian's concern is stewardship of the gospel." Efforts to promote peace, justice, and social standards may be labeled "social gospel," and moral issues like war, race, and ecology may be minimized and neglected because we believe the task of the church is "stewardship of the gospel."

Stewardship of the gospel does mean evangelism, winning people to Christ. But it also means helping them to grow in Christlikeness, in spiritual maturity. It means ministering to the needs of people, helping them to be physically, socially, and economically whole. It means dedicating our talents and all our resources to help accomplish these purposes.

A good friend of mine, Andrew Shelly, pointed out a number of years ago that we become greatly disturbed about the dangers of fallout from atomic tests, about the threat of atomic war, and about the evils of segregation. "We petition the president and the congress. We picket the White House. In moving oratory we point out the great cost in life and suffering and the effects upon persons yet unborn that these things will bring. Yet, at the same time, we possess great resources of wealth and we hold onto it while millions have never heard the gospel and when half the world is going to bed hungry.

"The possessions entrusted to us could feed the hungry of the world. It could give the gospel to the unevangelized. It does not cost much to cry out against the evils of war and of atomic tests, and there is not much we can do about them. But we can do something about the starving and the unevangelized. God has entrusted us with the means to do something. But this would cost us! We could not continue to indulge in luxuries, to get new cars every year or two. But, are we sure that the treasure that we hold back and do not share will not take greater toll than atomic tests? Are we sure that the dangers of nuclear war are greater than the avarice and greed of American Christians? Are we sure that the militarism of the nations is a graver threat to the peace and security of the world than the materialism of Christians?"

The stewardship of money is a vital part of stewardship of the gospel. It is evident that the moral, social, and economic areas of our lives are far from totally reconciled to God. In Christ, and through the ambassadors of Christ, God is still working to bring this about. We are stewards in promoting this purpose of God, stewards in helping people abound in the grace of giving.

10

STEWARDS OF
MATERIAL POSSESSIONS

God created a material world. He created a man of flesh and blood and asked him to be a steward of that world and to reap the material fruits of the earth. But man was more than a physical being, for God breathed into him the breath of life and he became a living soul. He was thus a spiritual being, capable of fellowship with the Creator. God wanted on the earth a people of flesh and blood to be a community of love and righteousness, a spiritual fellowship of human beings.

The fall of man has brought tension between the material and spiritual. Some men have tended to downgrade and deny the spiritual while others have downgraded and denied the material. Some Christians have a tendency to look with suspicion on material things, an inclination to find a monastical division between "secular" and "sacred," and to consider money as "mammon" or "filthy lucre."

One minister declared, "We make it a point never to mention money in our church." But this was not the attitude of our Lord nor of the Apostle Paul. Jesus said more about money and man's attitude toward it than any other thing. One may be amazed to find that the Bible re-

fers more to money and property relations than to anything else. Nearly 60 percent of the Bible deals with
these. "This is how gloriously materialistic the most spiritual Book is!" Jesus did not spend all His time talking
about the new birth, heaven, love, and righteousness. He
also talked much about material things and man's attitude
toward them.

Why Did Jesus Say So Much About Money?

Was Jesus money-minded? Was He trying to get all
He could? The answer is an emphatic "no." His main
concern was not for the poor or the good that money
can do, but rather for the wealthy and their need to
share and use it for kingdom purposes.

Jesus knew that it was hard for a rich man to enter
the kingdom. He knew that riches choke out the Word
and that a wrong attitude toward money could damn both
character and soul. He knew, on the other hand, that
sharing means blessing, enrichment of life, added opportunities and rewards, and treasures laid up in heaven.
He emphasized that it was more blessed to give than to
receive, and He wanted men to experience that blessedness.

Jesus asked people to share and to take the right
attitude toward money because He cared for people. He
was interested in their welfare. He did not want them
to get hurt but wanted them to experience the joy and
the blessing of generous giving. He wanted them to invest
in the great enterprises of God and receive rich dividends.
God asked His people to tithe, not for the sake of the
tithe, but for the sake of His people, "That the Lord
thy God may bless thee in all the work of thine hand
which thou doest" (Deut. 14:29).

One minister, in preparing a sermon on stewardship,

searched the Gospels to find what motives Jesus wanted people to have for giving. [1] He experienced two surprises. First, Jesus gave only one motive. The second surprise was the motive that Jesus offered. The motive was "sound investment." In other words, self-interest. "It is more blessed to give." "Give and it shall be given you." "Don't lay up treasures on the earth, for you will lose them; lay up your treasures in heaven where they will be safe and have eternal value." "Be good stewards and you will be made ruler over many things."

This may shock some, but why should it? If God is interested in our welfare, we should be too. Self-interest need not and must not be selfish. Selfishness destroys self-interest. Self-interest is a God-given instinct or drive. Like all instincts it can be abused, but to neglect or ignore it is also wrong and results in shriveled personalities.

God delights in blessing, prospering, and rewarding His people. He is "a rewarder of them that diligently seek him." To believe this is vital to the Christian faith (Heb. 11:6). We must believe in rewards here and in the hereafter. Dr. Carl Henry says, "The exclusion of final divine recompense as an element in contemplation of moral responsibility leads to incomplete and inadequate systems of ethics." [2]

When Is Money Mammon or Filthy Lucre?

With some people money, like sex, has a nasty and filthy connotation. This is unfortunate, for if rightly used both are sacred and good. Neither of these is bad or immoral in itself. Their use in the hands of bad and immoral men makes them evil. Money itself is harmless, a few metal coins or a bit of green paper. But persons who are covetous, greedy, miserly, and selfish often are guilty of committing economic immorality. They steal. They em-

145

bezzle. They hoard at the expense of the poor. They plunder and kill. They hold back what should be rendered to God for carrying out His purposes in the world. Money in the hands of unscrupulous men becomes mammon and filthy lucre.

"Mammon is money out of the control of God.

Mammon is money in mutiny — money seizing control over value.

Mammon is money in anarchy — money engaged in outlaw activities.

Mammon is money in atheism — money out of law and out of love." [3]

On the other hand, in the hands of a steward:

Money is missions, world evangelism.

Money is feeding the hungry, clothing the naked, housing the homeless.

Money is hospitals; care for the handicapped, the retarded, the mentally ill, the sick, and the aged.

Money is Bibles distributed, the gospel broadcast by radio and TV.

Money is young people trained for Christian service.

Money is glory to God, a sacrifice, a sweet-smelling savor.

Money is treasures laid up in heaven.

Money Must Be Brought Under the Lordship of Christ

No part of the Christian's life can be separated from Christian stewardship just as no part of his life can be separated from the lordship of Christ. Possessions are an important part of man's life. Money stands between more people and their relationship to God than any other one thing. For many reasons the stewardship of money is a vital part of the stewardship of the gospel.

Stewardship of money is vital because of the importance money holds in the lives and affections of people and the influence it has upon them. It is vital because of the tremendous dangers and penalties involved in the abuse and wrong use of money. It is vital because of the great potential for good of man and of the kingdom of God. Furthermore, it is important because our possessions really belong to God and have been entrusted to us for proper use. We must give an account before God how we use them.

We must try to rescue money from the mire of unscrupulous merchandising, from the quicksands of exploitation and riotous living, and from the corruption of hoarding and selfishness. We must transform it into currency of compassion and blessing, treasures laid up in heaven. Desecrated money can be a terrible blight on society and cause a world of misery and woe. Money consecrated and brought under the lordship of Christ can be tremendous power in promoting God's purposes on earth.

As Christians we must realize that the rich resources of the world are for all people of the world. Because "my land" happens to have oil wells, rich coal deposits, or other resources does not mean that only I should benefit from it, or that I may use the income selfishly, living in luxury while my neighbors suffer in poverty. Lawful possessions must not be regarded as merely our own but as God's gifts to others as well, administered by us. As our bank accounts and holdings grow, they should benefit others and God's kingdom as well as ourselves.

We are responsible for the use or misuse of the resources God has given the world. As we receive His gifts and as we follow justice and abound in charity, the necessities of life will be available for all. Man's selfishness, however, has made this impossible.

As we engage in earning, saving, spending, and managing money, we do so with the will of God and the promotion of His purposes in mind. To be dishonest and hurt people in earning money is bad stewardship even though we use the money earned for good purposes. To be industrious and frugal in earning and saving money is not good stewardship if we do so only to hoard it or use it for selfish purposes.

Money can be a mighty force to promote the will of God on earth. It can also have a devastating effect on the best interests of society and the kingdom of God. Money lost in the desert is useless. In wicked hands it becomes the devil's agent; in the hands of a Christian steward it becomes a power for God.

Stewards in Earning Money

Earning money or a living is a Christian's duty. He may earn by manual labor, by the use of his intellectual powers, or by a spiritual ministry. "They which preach the gospel should live of the gospel" (1 Cor. 9:14). The Scriptures tell us that if one does not provide for his own he has denied the faith and is worse than an infidel. Paul admonishes us to work with our hands so that we may have something to give. God expects man to be productive and to share. He has given man the power to get wealth. The Bible encourages industriousness and thrift and nowhere condones idleness or encourages poverty.

Poverty is no disgrace as long as a person is honestly doing what he can, but it is disgraceful to the one who loafs and squanders what he gets or tries to live off others. One may be sinfully poor as well as sinfully rich. On the other hand prosperity is no credit to the man who earns his money dishonestly and hoards it. Money is a credit to the Christian farmer, businessman, or laborer, provided it is earned honestly and used for the good of man and for the glory of God. Many Bible characters were God-fearing men yet had flocks, herds, servants, and riches. The riches of the world belong to God and He wants to share them with His servants. He wanted men to be prosperous. Sin and greed brought poverty into the world.

However, large amounts of money accumulated dishonestly and at the expense of others cannot please God. The great wealth of Solomon, one of the richest men in the world, was not an honor to God. To secure this wealth he exploited and made slaves of his people. He also greatly transgressed the commands of God in doing it. God had told Israel that when they possess the land and have a king, this king "shall not multiply horses to himself . . . neither shall he multiply wives to himself . . . neither shall he greatly multiply to himself silver and gold" (Deut. 17:14-17). Solomon did all of these and brought tragedy to the nation.

The Christian steward will ask a number of questions before entering a vocation to earn money. The first question will not be, "How big will the paycheck be?" Rather he will ask whether this will promote the welfare of man and the purposes of God. He will ask, Is it legal? Is it honest? Will it honor God? Because he is God's partner he cannot earn from enterprises contrary to the will of God or that are hurtful to others.

The saloon-keeper or bartender may be selling liquor at a legal price and have a state permit, yet he is helping to ruin lives, wreck homes, steep men, women, and children in poverty. He is helping cause 50 percent of our highway accidents and a large percent of the divorces in the United States. Tens of thousands of deaths are caused in America every year by alcohol.

The judge of a municipal court in Chicago declared,

"Booze is the mother of crime. It gives life and sustenance to slums, dives, gambling dens, and pay-off joints. It moves to his deed the homicide, the stick-up man, the burglar, the thief, and the thug. It fires the brain of the prostitute and the panhandler. . . . I have tried an army of 50,000 human derelicts, most of whom were booze-soaked." Surely no steward of God could work against the purposes of God by having anything to do with such a traffic.

The Bible pronounces many woes on covetous men who wrong their fellowmen in the pursuit of money. Jesus pronounced woes upon the Pharisees for pretending to be religious but were devouring widows' houses and omitting judgment and mercy. James says to the rich who have held back the wages of the laborers, "Go to now . . . weep and howl for your miseries that shall come upon you."

The Prophet Amos cried out against Israel because they "sold the righteous for silver, and the poor for a pair of shoes" (2:6). He charges, in chapter three, that their beautiful houses are full of loot from thefts and banditry. Micah charges Israel with driving widows from their homes and stripping children of every God-given right (2:2). One cannot love God, be a true steward of God, and treat his fellowmen thus. He will realize that his attitude toward people reflects his attitude toward God.

Tithes offered to God from excessive profits wrung from the poor or those of moderate circumstances will not bribe Him to overlook the injustice. Many ethical questions pop up as one discusses the matter of Christians making money. How much profit can a Christian make in his business and still remain Christian? If he is a professional man who can set his own charges how much can he charge and still be Christian in his practice? Can he serve people and charge at the rate of five times as much as the person he serves makes? Ten times as much? Bert Wilson, onetime secretary of the United Christian Missionary Union, raised some thought-provoking questions which we quote here.

"What is the boundary line between honest earnings and business shrewdness; between business shrewdness and covetousness; between covetousness and actual overreaching; between overreaching and unjust gain; between unjust gain and profiteering and theft? When does a man cease to be an honorable businessman and become a profiteer? Can the profiteer be a Christian? Why should government regulations allow operators of railroads only 6 percent profit on their investments and keep hands off many other industries, allowing them to reap a profit of 100 percent or even 1000 percent?"[4]

The person who takes excessive profits is a dangerous person. He is unfair to society and his profession. If he is a Christian, he brings reproach upon the church and his Lord. He is unfair to himself, exposing himself to the damning cancer of covetousness. Even if he gives generously to charities the injustice is not made right. Every steward in earning money should seek to honor God, be fair to his fellowmen, and maintain an upright character. Earning money for the support and comfort of his family, for the good of society, and for the furtherance of the cause of Christ is a legitimate goal. One may earn money in disgraceful ways, but it also can be God-honoring. Earning must never become an end in itself. We should ask, "For what purposes am I earning this money?"

Good Stewards in Saving Money

Before we get too excited, however, about saving

money we should answer the questions: What do we mean by saving? For what are we saving? By saving one may mean laying it up, storing it away, or hoarding it. This may be a vice instead of a virtue. Saving should never be an end in itself, but a means to a worthy end. Saving for the sake of saving is hoarding, and hoarding is sinful. It causes misery and makes misers of persons. Saving what should be spent or given for worthy causes shrivels the soul of the one who saves.

The rich fool evidently "saved" but is a striking example of a miserable steward. He made saving an end in itself. He saved until his barns would hold no more. He had far more than he could ever use while others were starving. He made no provision for his goods after he was gone. God told him his time was up and asked him, "Then whose shall those things be, which thou hast provided?" In that hour he was no better off than a beggar. What joy and satisfaction he could have had in life had he been a good steward of his possessions! What good his wealth could have done!

The rich, covetous man is self-centered and self-sufficient but nevertheless he is as surely a slave as the alcoholic and the drug addict. Money may be a wonderful servant but as a master it is a tyrant.

By saving we also may mean avoiding expense or waste. We may save by taking advantage of "specials," discount prices, or by buying a used car instead of a new one. We may save by economizing on home furnishings, foods, and vacations.

The Christian should try to avoid excessive and needless spending. He should save to promote worthy causes and to meet the needs of people. He may legitimately save to build up his business and to provide modest security. We must, however, realize the dangers and be careful that saving does not turn into covetousness and hoarding.

The Christian steward will not lay up large amounts of money which he can never use and which his heirs will not need. A. A. Hyde, the Mentholatum man of Wichita, believed it was not right to accumulate large amounts of money when there was so much need in the world. He saved what was needed to expand his business, but gave away the surplus. He believed it was wrong to save money so that children could live in luxury. He believed inherited money has damned thousands of heirs. He saved that he might be a liberal giver to Christian causes.

On one occasion when YMCA books were in the red, Mr. Hyde gave a signed check without filling in the amount. He stated what his bank balance was and that the check could be filled in for what was needed up to that amount. I am sure there are mission board treasurers and college presidents who would love to get some checks like that. Mr. Hyde saved to give. He gave hundreds of thousands to worthy causes.

John Wesley saved to give. His slogan was, "Earn all you can, save all you can, give all you can." This he practiced. When he was earning only thirty pounds, he lived on twenty-eight and gave away the rest. When he earned sixty pounds, he still lived on twenty-eight and gave away the rest. The next year his income was ninety pounds. He lived on twenty-eight, and gave away the remainder. When he got one hundred and twenty pounds, he lived on the same amount as before and gave away what was left. Later he gave up financial accounting and said, "It suffices that I gain all I can, I save all I can, and I give all I can, that is, all I have."

The example of the noted musician, Fritz Kreisler, should prick the consciences of Christians given to extravagant spending. He said, "I was born with music in my system. I knew musical scores instinctively before I knew my ABC's. It was a gift of providence. I did not acquire it. So I do not even deserve thanks for the music. Music is too sacred to be sold and the outrageous prices the music celebrities charge today are truly a crime against society. I never look upon the money I make as my own. It is public money. It is only a fund entrusted to my care for proper disbursement.

"I am constantly endeavoring to reduce my needs to a minimum. I feel morally guilty in ordering a costly meal, for it deprives someone else of a slice of bread — some child perhaps of a bottle of milk. My beloved wife feels the same way about things as I do. You know what I eat; you know what I wear. In all these years of so-called success in music we have never built a house of our own. Between it and us would stand all the homeless of the world."

A friend of mine feels much like Fritz Kreisler about spending and saving. He has never bought a new car for himself. Through some trusted dealer he can buy a good used car that will serve his purpose as well as a new one. In this way he can save a thousand dollars or more. Instead of paying $80 or $100 for a new suit, he can find what has been an expensive suit, slightly worn, for $5 or $10. Other family needs are met in the same way. He can save thousands of dollars annually to give to missions and relief. The joy of saving and giving exceeds the satisfaction of having new things. The treasures this man and his family lay up in heaven will exceed that of a half dozen average families with just as much income or more. Their earthly home may not be as lavishly furnished as the homes of their neighbors but more important, how will their heavenly homes compare?

These examples may seem extreme and radical to many of us. But we may ask, Are they extreme or are we extreme in the opposite way? What could be done for the needs of the world, for evangelism, and for ourselves if we followed these examples? How much greater would be our joy and meaning of life. Is our extravagant spending causing spiraling inflation and the cost of living which adds to the woes of the poverty-stricken people of the world? Are we permitting the world to form us into its mold of extravagance and self-indulgence? Does our saving and spending over the past year demonstrate good stewardship? Does it show responsible use of what God has entrusted to us? Are we saving to give?

Maybe we should look at the stubs of our checkbooks. What do they tell us about ourselves? Where has our money gone? How much have we given out of a heart of concern for missions? How much did we give compassionately for our suffering brothers and sisters at our doorsteps and around the world? Yes, the stubs of our checkbooks can tell us what kind of persons we are; whether we are stingy, self-indulgent individuals without compassion, or whether we are persons of faith, love, and charity. They can tell whether we serve God or mammon.

Tremendous pressure is being brought upon us today by advertisements and tempting TV commercials, urging us to buy what we do not need or could get along without. "Enjoy it now. Nothing down. Eighteen months to pay." And what a price some people pay for listening! In affluent times like these Christians are tempted to spend far too much on what is not really needed or to keep up with the Joneses. Then when there are crying needs on the mission fields or in famine-stricken lands they have little, or nothing, to give. Like Wesley, we should save to give.

We Are Stewards in Spending Money

"He is no fool who parts with what he cannot keep, to get what he cannot lose."

Since God gives us the possessions we have, He naturally is concerned about how we use them. He holds us accountable. As His stewards we will want our money to be used for the best purposes of God and society. The steward cannot squander what his Lord has entrusted to him. Surely he cannot use it against the purposes of God. He will see that a fair portion is given outright to the church and to the needs of his fellowmen. But he will be equally scrupulous in the use of the remainder, using it for the good of his family, of society, and as "unto the Lord."

Are Americans good stewards in spending money? One statistician told us some years ago that Christian people hold over half the wealth of America. Over 50 percent of the national income comes to church members. We are told that the projected total income for the nation in 1973 is to exceed a trillion dollars. A mere tithe of the share that comes to Christians would be over $50 billion. How the cause of missions, relief, and Christian philanthropy could go forward in 1973! In 1972 we approached the trillion dollar figure, but what did we do with it? December 25, 1972, *U.S. News and World Report* gives us an answer:

There's turning out to be big news in the way *people* are *spending money*. They're *loosening up* — spending more, saving less, living higher on the hog. . . . *More cars* will be bought this year than ever before — 10.8 million; still more — 11 million plus — in 1973. Six of ten are ordering air conditioning. *New homes* keep being built and bought in greater numbers than forecast. *Christmas* trade has taken off, as reported by merchants.

See page 26. *TV's* and *radios* are selling 20 percent faster than last year. Sales in *clothing* have jumped in all categories — especially *men's* wear. People are *eating better* on the average. The typical American has consumed 8 percent more *beef* this year than five years ago. And he's likely to down an even larger quantity in 1973, *despite complaints* over prices.

Page 26 tells us, "Shoppers are loosening their purse strings. Cash registers are ringing a happy tune. This holiday season is turning out to be an exceptionally rosy one." "All across the U.S. people have been flocking into stores of all sorts at a record rate. Predictions for a boom in holiday spending, forecast in recent months, may prove modest." "Unprecedented holiday-shopping totals now seem all but certain." "There is a trend toward expensive furnishings, appliances, expensive jewelry. Specialty shops report that more people are shopping for 'fun' items they really do not need."

Stores report that people buy more expensive items. One store exhausted its initial stock of $50 dolls and doll houses priced from $75 to $125. Another store reported that jewelry in the $300 to $400 range was selling extremely well. One company reported doing a good business in $11,000 houseboats, up 37 percent over last year's pre-Christmas sales.

Does this sound like responsible stewardship? How wonderful it would be if mission boards, relief agencies, and other Christian institutions could give a glowing report like this! Thank God, not everyone is forgetting these causes. Thousands of dollars in gifts will be given during the Christmas and year-end season by Christian stewards to the cause of Christ, whose birthday we pretend to celebrate. But how will His gifts compare with what we spend on ourselves? Should we not as Christians endeavor to give to Christian causes as much as the family spends on itself for Christmas? I know of one steward who has been doing this. Why not? After all, it is His birthday, the birthday of the King. Should we not have a gift for Him?

The morning I was writing this, the president of Hesston College came to his office, adjoining mine, and opened his mail. There were a number of letters from Christian stewards who were doing some year-end giving to the college, a check for $4,000, another for $2,000, and several checks for lesser amounts. No doubt other Christian institutions shared likewise from the generosity of God's stewards. Much as these gifts are appreciated, they are like the widow's two mites compared to what the crowds of Christmas shoppers spent on themselves and their families. No doubt the Lord would say, "These two mites are more than the gifts of the rich to their friends."

To spend money is not wrong. In fact, one may do wrong by not spending it. The Christian steward, concerned in promoting the purposes of his Lord, will carefully plan to spend what is entrusted to him. Money has value only as it is used. One may legitimately spend for his own needs, for the good and the happiness of his family, and for the welfare of others. But money lavished on one's self or his family needlessly is not for their good or happiness.

God gave Israel instructions to spend portions of their income. One tithe of the fruit of the ground and of the increase of their herds they were to give to the Levites. Another tithe they were to spend in connection with the festivals. Each third year they were to store up another tenth to share with the Levites, the stranger, the fatherless, and the widow. Not to spend this money as God directed was robbing God.

158

God Rebukes Selfish Spending

One of the great sins of Christians today is that of spending money lavishly upon themselves without regard for the needs of their fellowmen. God through the Prophet Amos rebukes Israel for this sin. "Woe to those lounging in luxury at Jerusalem and Samaria. . . . You lie on ivory beds surrounded with luxury, eating the meat of the tenderest lambs and choicest calves. . . . You drink wine by the bucketful and perfume yourselves with sweet ointments, caring nothing at all that your brothers need your help" (6:1-6, *Living Bible*). God says, "Therefore you will be the first to be taken as slaves; suddenly your revelry will end."

If God judged Israel for these sins, how can Christians of America escape — Christians who so accurately fit the description above. Affluence is making people callous to the needs of their fellowmen, just as it did in olden days. God is entrusting us with unprecedented wealth to promote His purposes, but God's stewards are misappropriating these funds and using them in sumptuous living. Someday God will call upon us to give account of our stewardship. The greatest tragedy in selfish spending, it seems to me, is not that the poor suffer, but rather what it does to the rich. They "fall into temptation and a snare, and into many foolish and hurtful lusts, which drown men in destruction and perdition." They miss the joy, the glory, and the blessing that could be theirs if they shared and were good stewards of God.

The Sin of Not Spending

Another great sin of which people are guilty today is hoarding, laying up treasures on the earth. Their sin is in not spending, not using wealth for the purposes God intended. Modest savings may be legitimate for Christians, but hoarding thousands upon thousands, which they can never use and which might curse their heirs, is wrong. Especially is this true when there is such great need in the world and the purposes of God are hindered for lack of funds.

God has given Christians of the Western world unprecedented wealth and affluence. If this wealth were dedicated to God it could do much for world evangelism and to help meet the needs of poverty-stricken people. Do we not sin against God, against society, and against ourselves if we use this selfishly or merely hoard it? Selfishly holding on to our possessions and not generously sharing are adding to the woes and the poverty of the world. Many of the ills of our society including war, violence, poverty, strikes, racism, rioting, alcoholism, drugs, and prostitution can be traced directly or indirectly to selfishness, covetousness, and the love of money, a root of all kinds of evil.

While Israel was in the wilderness God warned them that when He brought them into the promised land and gave them great and goodly cities which they did not build, houses full of good things that they did not fill, wells which they had not dug, vineyards and olive trees which they did not plant; and when they had eaten to the full, "Then beware lest thou forget the Lord, which brought thee forth out of the land of Egypt" (Deut. 6:10-12). Prosperity need not mean that people will forget the Lord and His work, but far too many people do fall into a snare when prosperity and wealth come to them. Spending freely for the kingdom of God and the welfare of mankind can save one from the cancer of covetousness.

Uncertain Riches

Paul tells Timothy to charge the rich not to trust in

uncertain riches. Riches have a way of getting away from people. We should practice stewardship while riches are in our hands. After the great Chicago fire three friends whose businesses had been wiped out by the fire met. One said, "Well, thank God there was some of my money placed where it could not burn." He walked away and cheerfully went about building up a new business. One of the two remaining men said to the other, "That man gave away nearly a million dollars last year, and if I had not been a fool I would have done the same."

Cash and Character

A noted Baptist minister declared, "A man wrong in money matters will be wrong in almost everything else. A man right in money matters will be right in everything else, or easily set right." There is much truth in that statement. A man who does not know how to earn money, save money, spend and give money, and how to manage money usually cannot manage his own passions and his life.

There is a close relationship between cash and character. The character of a man determines how he will spend his cash. Conversely, the way a man spends his money helps to determine his character. "What a young man earns during the day goes into his pockets; what he spends at night goes into his character." Someone suggested that nothing affects man's eyes as much as gold dust, and money often causes hardening of the attitudes.

Some people, like the prodigal spending his money in riotous living, use their cash to ruin their characters. Others, like the rich fool and Dives, use their cash to shrivel their characters by hoarding it. The more they get the more their characters shrivel. Still others, like the Good Samaritan and Zacchaeus, use their cash to enhance their characters. The more they have, the greater their characters, because they are good stewards in its use, helping their fellowmen and honoring God.

A man with a miserly character will hoard his money at the expense of his fellowmen and of the kingdom of God. A profligate character will squander his Lord's money to his own hurt and to the hurt of society. A thievish character will steal from others, rob, and kill that he may have more. The covetous character will defraud and exploit people for his own profit. On the other hand, the generous character will render tithes and offerings for the work of Christ's kingdom and for the good of his fellowmen. The man of compassion, like the Good Samaritan, will share his money and his talents to minister to others. The man with Christian character will seek first the kingdom of God rather than selfish purposes.

Money, a Friend or Foe?

Money! Money! What a phenomenon! What a paradox!

Money is a joy to the steward, a friend of the needy, a grace to the giver, a helper to the servant. It is a great blessing to man.

Money is a snare to the covetous, an evil to the miser, an enemy of the spendthrift, the master of the lover of money. It is a great curse to man.

Money can serve man or rule him. Money can be a blessing or a curse, can enrich or impoverish man, can be man's friend or his enemy, can improve man or ruin him, can mean treasures in heaven or it can mean perdition, can enhance personality or shrivel it, can make man or break him. Money can mean life or it can mean death.

No wonder our Lord was interested in man and money. No wonder He said, "Make to yourselves friends of the mammon of unrighteousness."

11

THE GRACE OF GIVING

Giving Is Living

"For giving is living," the angel said,
"Go feed to the hungry sweet charity's bread."

"And must I keep giving again and again?"
My selfish and querulous answer ran.

"Oh, no!" said the angel, piercing me through;
"Just give 'til the Master stops giving to you!"

It was E. Stanley Jones, I believe, who said, "There is no abundant living without abundant giving." Our God is a giving God. He so loves that He gives. He is the giver of life, the giver of every good and perfect gift. He gave His Son that we might be redeemed, and He freely gives us all things. He has given us His Word and His Spirit.

God deeply ingrained in His creation the law of giving. He created the sun to give light, the fruit trees to give fruit. The clouds give rain; the birds give their song; the flowers give their beauty and fragrance; the bees give us honey; the cows give milk; the sheep give their wool. Greatest of all, Jesus gave His life a ransom for all — the

163

gift of eternal life.

What a wretched world this would be if everything stopped giving! Life itself would cease. Christian giving means life, joy, blessing, and growth. Withholding leads to poverty, joylessness, frustration, and failure. The man who tries to save his life loses it, but the one who gladly gives his life finds it. God created man to be self-giving and generous. Sin made him self-loving and covetous. Only as man is reconciled to God and has the love of God in his heart can he experience the abundant life, the life of giving and sharing.

Why Emphasize Giving?

God taught the Hebrews to give. Jesus taught His followers to give. The Christian church has always taught sharing and giving. But Christians today, by and large, give far below scriptural standards. This practice dishonors God, hinders the work of Christ's kingdom, and brings reproach upon the church. It fosters covetousness, envy, and hate. It impoverishes the characters and souls of those who withhold their giving.

The primary desire of the Christian steward is to do God's will and promote His purposes in the world. These purposes are to reconcile the world to Himself and to form a community of love and righteousness. To this end the faithful steward will gladly use his talents and give generously of his means. Generous giving will be inevitable and spontaneous when one has had a vital experience with God and understands God's great purposes for His people and when he understands what God has done, is doing, and will still do for His people.

1. The Christian steward will give generously because that is God's will for him. "God loveth a cheerful giver." Generous gifts are "an odour of a sweet smell, a sacrifice

acceptable, wellpleasing to God" (Phil. 4:18). Helping others and sharing are "the kind of sacrifice that gives God joy" (Heb. 13:16, Laubach). Paul tells the Corinthians that the reason he is collecting aid for the Christians at Jerusalem is that it brings glory to God (2 Cor. 8:19, Laubach).

2. We will give generously because giving is required in the Scriptures. The principle of material giving to God consistently runs throughout the Bible. When man gives, he is blessed of God. When he withholds, he is cursed because he is robbing God. The Scriptures emphasize this truth frequently in the history of Israel. Jesus constantly taught that giving means blessing.

In the Old Testament God asked for sacrifices, for the firstfruits and the firstlings, for freewill offerings, for the tithes from the flocks and herds, and from the fruit of the fields. As three times a year the Hebrews went to Jerusalem for the feasts they were not to go empty-handed, but were to give as God prospered (Deut. 16:16, 17).

In the New Testament Jesus says, "Give, and it shall be given unto you." He tells us to lay up treasures in heaven. The Apostle Paul also emphasized giving. "He that gives let him do it with a big heart. . . . Give to the saints who need help" (Rom. 12:8, 13). He told Timothy to charge the rich to use their money to do good, to be rich in good works, and generous in sharing (1 Tim. 6:18). He asked the churches in Galatia and at Corinth to set aside on the first day of the week as God prospered (1 Cor. 16:1, 2).

3. We will give generously because of God's great promises. Paul told the Corinthians not to let fear of the future keep them from being generous, for God is able to give more than we need and will give us enough that we can give to every good cause (2 Cor. 9:8, Laubach). If we

take seriously God's promises, we will not let fear of the future keep us from giving generously. With faith in God's promises the Macedonians gave when in deep poverty. The poor widow gave all her living. The widow of Zarephath because of her faith gave her last meal and oil to the Prophet Elijah. We can be sure that none of these suffered for having done what they did. Their faith and dedication were richly rewarded.

But Jesus makes some rather fantastic statements, unbelievable to men of little faith. "It is more blessed to give than to receive." What mortal man can believe that? Yet, no one has ever accepted that philosophy and faithfully practiced it without discovering its truth. It was our Lord Himself who made that statement, and if anyone knew the truth of it surely it would be Jesus, for no one else ever gave as He gave.

Another statement of Jesus, "Give, and it shall be given unto you; good measure, pressed down, and shaken together, and running over. . . . For with the same measure that ye mete withal it shall be measured to you again." What hard-headed businessman would ever accept that philosophy and practice it? But again, he who disregards the teachings of Jesus is the loser.

Some years ago a man in Michigan started out with $1.50. Two decades later he was operating one of the largest service station businesses in the state. He was called to a White House Conference on small businesses. They wanted to know how he had done this. What was the secret? He said that he just tried to give away more than his competitors did. It was not stamps, prizes, or chances he gave away, but service. After snowstorms he plowed driveways for people, picked up grocery orders, met unexpected guests at the airport, anything to help his customers, all without charge.

When an important executive asked him where he got the idea, he pointed to an old worn Bible. "It belonged to my dad," he said, "and I try to run my business by this passage: 'Give, and it shall be given unto you: good measure, pressed down, shaken together, and running over. . . . For with the same measure that ye mete withal it shall be measured to you again.'" He had started by giving away gratis free parking space, up-to-date delivery of workers' cars in bad weather. Jesus' teaching held true for the service station owner. It will hold true for any Christian who has enough faith to try it.

4. Our love and compassion compels us to give generously to the needs of our brethren and for carrying out the Great Commission of our Lord. "The love of Christ constraineth us." Seeing our brothers in need we cannot shut our heart of compassion against them. It is a startling statement, but I believe true that the size of our gifts to God, in proportion to His gifts to us, is the measure of our love and compassion.

Great suffering and poverty exist in the world as well as great need for world evangelism. God has given us our abilities and possessions to be partners with Him in meeting these needs. We cannot have a true sense of stewardship without responding generously. The flimsy excuse that we cannot afford to give the tithe or give generously when our income is in the upper fourth or eighth of the people of the world does not make good stewardship sense. Usually it is not lack of funds that keeps one from giving.

Bishop Asariah of India said, "Inadequate giving is due in the first place to lack of spiritual vigor. Christians do not give their money to God because they have not first given themselves to God. A proper recognition that all that we have belongs to God, that we have been bought with a price, the price being nothing less than the 'precious blood of Christ,' and that nothing we can give is adequate to recompense for such love is what is lacking in most people. The low ratio of giving is a symptom of the low level of Christian life. The sooner we recognize this the better."

Some years ago I read the statement that more people go to hell because of lack of funds than for any other reason. For years I served on the executive committee of our mission board. Far too often when there was an opportunity for expansion of the work or more personnel was needed on the field the answer was "insufficient funds." Might the real answer have been "insufficient love, compassion, and commitment"?

6. We give generously because of the blessings involved — blessings to others, blessings to ourselves, and glory to God. "Your generous gift through me will make many people thank God for you. Generous giving works that way. You will do more than take care of the needs of God's people in Jerusalem; you will also produce an outpouring of praises to God. And more than that, your giving will prove that your religion is real. If you make a generous gift to them and to others everyone will thank God and say: 'These Christians not only believe in Christ, they also practice what they believe'" (2 Cor. 9:11-13, Laubach).

The millions given each year by Christians for the suffering people of the world and for the proclamation of the gospel bring untold blessing to many. It is a sacrifice, well-pleasing to God. But perhaps the greatest blessing is to the givers. It is interesting to note the Scriptures that urge giving. The emphasis is never on the gift, not even on the needy persons. It is for the sake of the giver. Let us notice a few verses as paraphrased in *The Living Bible*:

Prov. 3:9, 10: "Honor the Lord by giving him the first part of all your income, and he will fill your barns with wheat and barley and overflow your wine vats with the finest wines."

Deut. 14:28, 29: "Every third year you are to use your entire tithe for local welfare programs: Give it to the Levites who have no inheritance among you, or to foreigners, or to widows and orphans within your city, so that they can eat and be satisfied; and then Jehovah your God will bless you and your work."

Mal. 3:10: "Bring all the tithes into the storehouse so that there will be food enough in my Temple; if you do, I will open up the windows of heaven for you and pour out a blessing so great you won't have room enough to take it in!"

We have already noticed the statements of Jesus, "Give, and it shall be given you," and "It is more blessed to give."

Paul says, "Sow bountifully and you will reap bountifully."

Note also 1 Tim. 6:18, 19: "Tell them to use their money to do good. They should be rich in good works and should give happily to those in need, always being ready to share with others whatever God has given them. By doing this they will be storing up real treasure for themselves in heaven — it is the only safe investment for eternity! And they will be living a fruitful Christian life down here as well."

Many other Scriptures could be given. God's heart longs to bless and prosper His people. His purpose in asking us to give is not that He needs it for Himself, but because He wants us to be His stewards to promote His work and to know the joys and blessings of sharing.

How Do We Give?

As Christians we would like to be considered good and generous. We want to do our part. On the other hand, we also desire to possess and to feel secure. We like to have new cars, new furniture, and new gadgets. We cannot get these things for ourselves with the dollars we give to missions. What is given to Christian colleges cannot be used for buying a new carpet. We cannot get T-bone steaks with the money we give to feed the world's hungry. We would like to give to Christian causes, but we would like also to have these things. This conflict causes us to ask, How do we give? There are different kinds of givers.

Some of us are "dream givers." Giving to missions, feeding the poor, and supporting the church have a great appeal to us. But we also want many things we do not have, and after all, we are not as wealthy as some. If we have an increase in income we get some things we have wanted but could not afford. To ease our consciences we imagine what large gifts we would give if only we were rich. We hope someday to make substantial contributions, but we are not now giving what we could be giving. We are dream givers. Dream giving feeds no hungry people, supports no missions, helps no worthy students through college.

Some of us are generous with other people's money. We salve our consciences by thinking and telling how we would give if we had the money that our neighbors have. If we had money like Mr. Ford has we would give much more than he is giving to Christian colleges and hospitals through the Ford Foundation. We hope sometime to be wealthy so that we can afford to give generously. Yet we give very little of what we earn, even though we have a greater income than three fourths of the people of the world. Thinking how generous we would be if we were wealthy supports no missionary. It endows no college. It builds no new church buildings.

Others of us are "yes" givers. We give when asked to do so. It is easier for us to say "yes" than it is to say "no." Often we would prefer using the money in some other way, but when asked to give we cannot refuse. We even complain if the solicitor misses us. "Why didn't he call on me? I had a check ready." But we do not send the check in voluntarily. If not asked to give, we do not give.

Then some of us are "special givers." We contribute little to the regular offering or to the church budget. We like to support special causes, causes that appeal to us. This kind of giver has done much good and has supported many worthy causes, but as far as his own church is concerned he is a hitchhiker. It would be difficult to have an effective church program if all givers were of this type.

Fortunately some of us are proportionate givers. Regularly we render our tithes to the Lord and find much satisfaction and profit in the practice. These givers are quite different from the ones mentioned before; they give without being asked to do so. They do not try to justify themselves for not giving, for they have set aside a portion to give. Usually they are regular supporters of the church budget and do even more than their share. They consider giving a joyous privilege and recognize their obligation to give to God and the church whether they have little or much.

The consistent proportionate giver will not stop at the tithe, however. As his income increases he will go beyond the tenth. Many find greater joy in giving 20 percent, 30 percent, or more. They give to God according to His gifts to them.

Finally, a few are sacrificial givers who actually deny themselves in order that others may have and give liberally to the cause of Christ. The widow casting in her two mites is an example. She cast in her living. A Korean father and son plowed their land by hand because they had sold their ox so they could have money to give for a new church.

A girl in the East some time ago suggested to her mother that they put up a while longer with their worn-out davenport in order to give to a needy cause their hard-earned money which they had saved for a new davenport. This kind of giver God loves.

Someone has said that in the awful struggle between good and evil — between God and the evil one — money is the weapon. We help one side or the other by the way we use money. "God loveth a cheerful giver," literally, "an hilarious giver."

Some Bible Examples of Giving

Cain and Abel (Gen. 4:2-4). Cain offered to God "of the fruit of the ground," not firstfruits. Abel offered "the firstlings of the flock," a greater sacrifice. The duty of rendering to God was recognized in the earliest days.

Abraham (Gen. 14:20; Heb. 7:4). Abraham offered tithes to the priest of the Most High. This suggests that the principle of the tithe was observed hundreds of years before the Mosaic law was given.

Jacob (Gen. 28:22). Out of gratitude for what God had promised to do for him, Jacob vowed to give to God a tenth of all that God would give him.

The Israelites for the work of the tabernacle (Ex. 35, 36). Here is an interesting story, not too often duplicated by the church. Moses asked the children of Israel to bring freewill offerings for the construction of the tabernacle. The people responded so liberally that the workers came to Moses and said, "The people bring much more

172

than enough." Moses commanded that the people bring no more offering for the sanctuary. Can you imagine the joy in the hearts of pastors and building committee chairmen if this happened when a new church building is needed?

The construction of the temple (1 Chron. 29:1-14). King David had contributed thousands of talents of gold and silver and other materials in abundance for the work of the temple. He then asked all who were of a willing heart to give. The rulers and leaders responded generously and "with perfect heart they offered willingly." The generous response caused great joy. "Then the people rejoiced . . . and David the king also rejoiced with great joy. Wherefore David blessed the Lord before all the congregation."

Generous giving always opens the springs of joy. God's people cannot be the joyous people He wants them to be when they fail to render their tithes and offerings and to respond to the needs of people and of the kingdom. Two percent or five percent of our income will not suffice to keep the springs of joy open. It represents too little faith, too little gratitude, and too little commitment.

Zacchaeus (Lk. 19:1-8). In the times of Jesus the practice of giving alms, tithing, and giving to the temple treasury was common among the Jews. Tithing of the smallest seeds, mint, dill, and cummin though common was not always accompanied by justice, mercy, and truth.

Zacchaeus, a prominent official in the Roman Customs Department, said to Jesus, "Lord, the half of my goods I give to the poor; and if I have defrauded any one of anything, I restore it fourfold." His decision to put his money matters straight brought this man the assurance from the Lord: "Today salvation has come to this house." His conversion reached to his pocketbook as does every genuine conversion.

The poor widow (Mk. 12:41-44). "And Jesus sat over

against the treasury and beheld how the people cast money into the treasury; and many that were rich cast in much." Then the poor widow came along and threw in two small coins. The Lord was delighted and remarked to His disciples that this woman had given more than the rich had given, for she gave her living. Several things in this story bother some people.

First, how could Jesus do such a thing as sit there and watch how much people give and then make remarks about their giving? He did this because of His deep interest in people and because He knew that their giving was an indication of the condition of their hearts. He felt concern for the covetous who were shriveling their souls. He rejoiced with those who knew the joy of sharing.

We can be sure that the Lord watches today as the offering is being received in our churches. He sees the generous gifts, perhaps small in amount but given sacrificially, and rejoices because here are persons who are reaping bountifully. He sees the gifts given grudgingly, gifts small in comparison to what God has given. He sees that withholding tends to poverty of soul.

Second, how could Jesus let her give her last cent? Had He no feelings? Some might have said, "Woman, you can't do that. You have to live." Jesus knew that the principle, "It is more blessed to give than to receive," was true. Her "bread cast on the waters" would return manyfold. We should never discourage the poor from giving. They are the ones who need the blessings that are sure to come when in faith they honor God.

Years ago a poor Hindu in Nepal was offering some rice to his god. He had not enough rice for his family. Someone said to him, "You must not do that. You have to live." His answer was, "No, I don't have to live, but I have to worship."

Third, by what stretch of the imagination could Jesus say that her two mites were more than the large gifts of the rich. We are inclined to widely publicize the large gifts that come to the church and scarcely notice the smaller gifts, even though they may represent more sacrifice and dedication than the larger ones. Jesus appraised the gifts not by the amount given, but by the amount remaining.

The example of the early church (Acts 2:44, 45; 4:32-37). The disciples, after being filled and empowered by the Holy Spirit, realized that what they had was not their own. They sold possessions and laid the price at the apostles' feet. None lacked, and they had "all things common." Barnabas is given as an example. He had a field and sold it and gave the proceeds to the apostles.

The churches of Macedonia (2 Cor. 8:1-5). These churches, out of deep poverty, gave generously to the needy in Judea. Paul says they were poor and had suffered greatly, yet they were full of joy. Their own need made them anxious to give help to Jerusalem's need. "They gave it of their own free will. In fact, they begged us for the favor of letting them have a part in the relief of God's people" (Laubach). Paul uses the example of these churches to challenge the church of Corinth to give to the needs of God's people.

The Philippians supply Paul's needs (Phil. 4:10-19). Paul writes to these Christians to thank them for sharing with him while he is in prison. He says that they had ministered to him once and again. "No church communicated with me as concerning giving and receiving, but ye only." He tells them the things they sent were "an odour of a sweet smell, a sacrifice acceptable, wellpleasing to God." He assures them that God will supply all their needs.

He no doubt is referring to the church at Philippi when he tells the Corinthians (2 Cor. 11:8, 9, TEV): "While I was working among you I was paid by other churches. I was robbing them, so to speak, to help you. . . . The brothers who came from Macedonia brought me everything I needed." He refers to their giving ministry as "fellowshipping in the gospel."

These examples of the way God's people gave indicate that generous giving brings rejoicing and satisfaction to the giver. It results in honor, praises, and thanksgiving to God. It calls forth the commendation and blessings from God. Finally, it helps bring relief to needy people and promotes the spread of the gospel. No wonder Jesus said, "It is more blessed to give than to receive."

How Much Should I Give?

To the Corinthians, Paul wrote, "Yet each person must make up his own mind what he will give. He must not be pushed or compelled to give. God loves the man that is happy when he gives. But do not let fear of the future prevent you from being generous" (2 Cor. 9:7, 8, Laubach). Fine! Then it is left to me, but how do I make up my mind? Do I give what is left after I have met all my wants? Do I decide on the whim of the moment? Or, do I gauge my giving by what others give? Maybe it would be fair if I gave my share of the suggested quotas of my congregation.

Suppose that I am a man with an income of around $10,000 a year and four in the family. As stewards of God our primary interest is in promoting God's purpose in the world. I believe that the money I have as well as my talents is a trust from God to be used wisely. Of the $10,000 how much should be given outright for kingdom purposes? Does divine revelation have the answer for me?

The Old Testament Answer

We have noticed that Abraham and Jacob gave the tithe. The law of Moses demanded that the Hebrews give tithes of the herds and of the fields. There is evidence that the Jews gave two tithes annually and a third tithe every third year. This would mean giving 20-25 percent. On special occasions they were also asked for offerings to which they responded generously.

How could Israel afford it? The fact is Israel could not afford not to. Eight tenths with the blessings of God was far more than ten tenths without God's blessing. It does not make good sense to the man of the world, but it does make good stewardship sense. When God told Israel to give a tithe of all, He said, "That the Lord thy God may bless thee in all the work of thine hand which thou doest" (Deut. 14:29). We see in Malachi the result of unfaithfulness. God accused Israel of robbing Him by not rendering tithes and offerings. He challenged them to bring again the tithes and offerings and see whether things would not be different.

The New Testament Answer

Jesus warned against serving mammon and against laying up treasures on the earth. He told the rich young ruler to sell all he had and give it away if he wanted eternal life. He commended the widow for giving her all. Seemingly He was delighted when Zacchaeus told Him that he would give half his goods to feed the poor. Jesus Himself gave His all.

Paul instructs the churches that "everyone" should give. They should do it regularly, "The first day of the week." They were to give proportionately "as God prospered." Their giving was to be in proportion to God's gifts to them. Could this furnish a standard for us? "Give as God prospers." Would it affect our giving if we knew that God would give in proportion to what we give? What would our income be if God gave us ten times what we give to Him? Would we have more? Or would we starve? But isn't this what the New Testament teaches us? Give in proportion to God's gifts to us.

Perhaps we cannot establish a definite percent from the New Testament. Some, however, believe strongly that the Scriptures do set the standard, tithes and offerings. Personally I have come to believe that while the tithe may have been a good standard under the law and may serve today as minimum standard, it is not adequate for the Christian in an affluent society.

We give according as God has given us. The amount may not be a fixed amount; it may have a floor but not a ceiling. When we give according to God's gifts to us, the amount will be determined by the measure of our gratitude, our love, our compassion, and our commitment. The amount we give will be determined by the warmth of our love and appreciation and not by a percent of cold cash we receive.

How Do I Make Up My Mind What to Give?

So each one of us makes up his own mind. As stewards of God what are some factors to reckon with as we make up our minds? I cannot answer that for you, but I can answer it for myself. My faith would tell me that "He who wills to do His will shall know" applies here. Here are other considerations:

1. Jesus and New Testament writers lowered no moral or spiritual standards. Grace stands high above law in every way. No way, therefore, could I accept a standard lower than the law. The tithe would be absolute bottom. Love in fulfilling the law would never sink below the law. One man

178

stated it something as follows: "When it comes to the tithe I am not under the law, but if I accept a standard lower than the law neither am I under grace; I am under disgrace."

2. I try to remember the grace of the Lord Jesus who was rich but became poor for my sake that I might be rich. As I am grateful for what He has done for me and appreciate His riches, and as I sense His concern for a lost and needy world, I must become generous in giving, even willing to become poor that others may share the Lord's riches. When I consider His gifts to me and the pressing needs of His cause, I would feel quite uncomfortable giving only the tithe in this time of American affluence.

I feel a great deal of agreement with a pastor who wrote me recently. He said we must stop preaching the tithe. In these days most of our churches could and should give an average of 20 percent per member. He is practicing what he is preaching and an increasing number of Christians are beginning to share the conviction and are being blessed for it. Personally, I will have an uneasy conscience if in my 1973 income tax report my contributions to the church and Christ's kingdom are below 20 percent, if God continues to prosper as He now is.

3. Some startling statistics should help us make up our minds to give generously. Ten thousand persons died today because of inadequate food. One billion, almost a third of the world's population, are physically or mentally retarded because of poor diet. The average income of a person in India is $60 per year; in the United States it is about $3,500.

America with 6 percent of the world's population consumes nearly 50 percent of the commodities and is responsible for about 50 percent of the world's pollution.

In 84 countries of the world people exist on less than $200 a year. In 37 of these countries the per capita income is less than $100 per year. The average American consumes 1,455 pounds of food per year, and we pay millions of dollars for pills to fight obesity. If the food available in India was distributed at the rate Americans eat, 153 million Indians would starve.

I read recently that the increase of the Gross National Product of America exceeds the total GNP of Africa. These are some cruel facts that should give us real concern, if not from the viewpoint of compassion, then from the viewpoint of our own welfare. How long will 90 percent of the people permit less than 10 percent to splurge in luxury, exploit and consume 50 percent of the world's resources and possess half the capital of the world?

Abundant evidence indicates that people and nations are getting impatient about our affluence. There are many rumblings to "share the wealth." The few with the wealth will not stand much chance when the underprivileged decide to take things in hand. A church bulletin recently carried this insert: "If the rich keep considering their wealth as a right, the poor will consider their vengeance as justice."

It is my strong conviction that selfishly hanging on to our wealth will eventually cause our doom. If Christians of America would give 20 to 30 percent of their income to meet church and world needs it would be the best investment they could make. It could prove even to be a good investment for them economically. In the light of world needs and in view of the affluence of the people of America, how could a committed Christian justify giving only a tithe of his income?

12

STEWARDSHIP AND THE TITHE

Since the primary concern of the Christian steward is to promote God's purposes in the world, he must dedicate himself and his possessions to those purposes. The needs of the steward, of his family, as well as the needs of the church and of the world must be considered as part of his stewardship. All of these are included in the interests of God.

A vital question to the faithful steward will be how much of his income should he spend on himself and family and how much for the work of the church and the needs of the world. How can he use wealth entrusted to him to best serve God's kingdom? Does this call for the tithe of his income for kingdom purposes? Is the Christian obligated to render tithes as Israel was required to do to promote the Hebrew society? Would this be a fair and adequate amount for a Christian steward to give? This question has been discussed pro and con almost since the inception of the Christian church.

By Christian tithing is meant the practice of regularly setting aside at least a tenth of one's income for kingdom purposes. One does so in grateful response to God's love

181

because he recognizes God as Owner of all things, including himself. Those who practice and advocate giving a tithe or more than the tithe are persons who have given it a fair trial and found it a joyful experience; those who reject it usually are those who have never given it a fair trial. Few exceptions will be found to this statement.

The Tithe in History

While there is no way of knowing for certain the origin of the tithe, some believe it was a law of God from the beginning, at least after the failure of Adam and Eve to recognize divine ownership in the garden. The purpose of the tithe was to help man recognize God's ownership and man's stewardship.

Some early churchmen, as well as later Bible students, believe there may be an allusion to the practice of tithing in the offerings of Cain and Abel. Abel brought the firstlings of the flock while Cain merely brought "of the fruit of the ground," not "first fruits." In the Septuagint version of the Old Testament God says to Cain, "If thou hast offered aright but hast not divided aright, hast thou not sinned?"

The writer of Hebrews says Abel offered to God "a more excellent sacrifice." Thayer translates it "greater in quantity." Some of the church fathers — Tertullian, Clement of Rome, and Irenaeus — believed that Cain offered rightly but did not offer proportionately; he cheated God. Some Bible scholars hold that the firstfruits and firstlings were identical with the tithes. If this interpretation of Cain and Abel is correct, the law of the tithe was in effect at the time of Cain.

At any rate, the practice of tithing preceded Moses by hundreds of years. We are told by good authority that there is evidence of the prevalence of tithing among the ancient Egyptians, East Indians, Babylonians, Assyrians, ancient Chinese, and other early nations. The historian, Moracutius, declares, "Instances are mentioned in history of some nations who did not offer sacrifices, but in the annals of all times none are found who did not pay tithes." In the light of this, one must ask why did all these peoples practice tithing? It would seem that either God commanded it from the beginning or there was a universal innate sense of obligation to God. Either would argue for an early revelation from God in regard to the tithe.

The example in the Old Testament of Abram paying tithes of all to the priest of the Most High God (Gen. 14) and Jacob vowing to give a tenth of all to God (Gen. 28) is well known. Professor Sayce says that in offering tithes Abram was doing nothing new, that he was long familiar with the practice in his Babylonian home. He states that there are in the British Museum many receipts of tithe money paid to the sun god by Chaldeans of Abram's day.

The Tithe Under the Law

Both internal and external evidences indicate that under the law the Hebrews paid two tithes every year and another tithe every third year.

The tithe is first required in Leviticus 27:30-33 (*The Living Bible*):

> "A tenth of the produce of the land, whether grain or fruit, is the Lord's and is holy. If anyone wants to buy back this fruit or grain, he must add a fifth to its value. And the Lord owns every tenth animal of your herds and flocks and other domestic animals, as they pass by for counting. The tenth given to the Lord shall not be selected on the basis of whether it is good or bad, and there shall be no substitutions."

According to this passage the tithe of both the produce

of the land and of the herd was holy to the Lord. The tithe of the seed and fruit could be redeemed by paying a fifth more. But the tithe of the animals could not be redeemed. This tithe is mentioned in Numbers 18:21-26. In this passage God tells the Levites that they are to give to the Lord a tenth of the tithes that they receive.

The second tithe is recorded in Deuteronomy 14:22-27 (*The Living Bible*):

> "You must tithe all of your crops every year. Bring this tithe to eat before the Lord your God at the place he shall choose as his sanctuary; this applies to your tithes of grain, new wine, olive oil, and the firstborn of your flocks and herds. The purpose of tithing is to teach you always to put God first in your lives."

God tells them that if the distance to His sanctuary is too great they may sell the grain and animals and take the money and buy what they want at the place of the sanctuary, "An ox, a sheep, some wine, or some strong drink to feast there before the Lord your God, and to rejoice with your household." They were not to forget to share their income with the Levites of their community.

This is known as the festival tithe and was to be given "year by year." The purpose of the tithe was to teach His people always to put God first in their lives and was to be a joyful occasion, a time of celebration.

In Deuteronomy 14:28, 29 is recorded the instructions for the third tithe. At the end of three years Israel was to bring all the tithes of their increase and lay them up to give to the Levites, the foreigners, the widows and orphans within their cities that they might eat and be satisfied, "that the Lord thy God may bless thee in all the work of thine hand which thou doest."

Some believe this to be the same tithe as the "festival

184

tithe" but each third year given to the Levite, the stranger, and the needy instead of being eaten by the offerer and his family, as was the case the other two years. In the apocryphal book of Tobit, written nearly two hundred years before Christ, we read:

"The first tenth of all increase I gave to the sons of Aaron: another tenth part I sold away, and went, and spent it every year at Jerusalem: and the third I gave to whom it was meet."[1]

This would indicate that the Jews paid three tithes. Josephus likewise mentions three tithes, two every year and another every third year:

"Besides the two tenths, which I have already said you are to pay every year, the one for the Levites, the other for the festivals; you are to bring every third year a third tithe to be distributed to those that want; to women who are widows; and to children that are orphans."[2]

Israel's Failure

Israel miserably failed in consistent payment of the tithe to the Lord. As they disregarded the obligation, tragedy overtook them. However, at each great spiritual awakening the payment of the tithe was one of the first reforms. We notice this under Hezekiah and again under Nehemiah. The remnant that returned with Nehemiah retrogressed and lost out on the tithe. Malachi upbraids them in the following words:

"You have robbed me of the tithes and offerings due to me. And so the awesome curse of God is cursing you, for your whole nation has been robbing me. Bring all the tithes into the storehouse so that there will be food enough in my Temple, and if you do I will open up the windows of heaven for you and pour out a blessing so great you won't have room enough to take it in.

"Try it! Let me prove it to you! Your crops will be large, for I will guard them from insects and plagues. Your grapes won't shrivel away before they ripen, says the Lord of Hosts. And all nations will call you blessed, for you will be a land sparkling with happiness. These are the promises of the Lord of Hosts."[3]

This message of Israel's failure, God's complaint against His people for omitting the tithe, and His promise to bless them if they would renew the observance of this command, is found in the last chapters of the Old Testament. In the beginning chapters of the Old Testament we have the charge of stewardship given to man, and the record of the first sin as man failed to recognize God's ownership and man's stewardship.

In the last chapters of the Old Testament God's people are in tragic circumstances because they disregarded God's ownership. The closing rebuke, challenge, and call of God to His people was a rebuke for being unfaithful stewards. God challenged them to faithfulness in rendering to Him the things that are His. Man's failure was the failure to love and obey his Creator and to be a good steward of material things entrusted to him by his Maker.

Four hundred years later the Messiah came. He was a perfect example of Christian stewardship. By precept and example He taught man what the Father from the beginning expected of man. He was about His Father's business and sought first the kingdom of God. He kept the commandments of God and taught men to render to God what is God's. He made it clear that man must give to live. To find life abundant one must lose himself in the interests of others and of the kingdom. He warned His followers of the dangers of covetousness. He recognized the vital relationship of the proper use of possessions to the Christian personality.

Jesus and the Tithe

If tithing is for the Christian, why have we so little in the New Testament on the subject? Why did Jesus say so little about the tithe? Jesus said little about rendering tithes or observing the Sabbath. The Jews of Jesus' day were meticulous in keeping both the tithe and the Sabbath. In fact, they were inclined to overemphasize them, to make them ends in themselves. Jesus did not have to preach keeping the Sabbath or payment of the tithe; they were religiously doing both.

Jesus, however, did say more about possessions and attitudes toward possessions than about anything else. His teachings, if kept, would never lead one to give less than the tithe of the Old Testament, or less than the Jew gave under the law. Nowhere does He say a word that would indicate abrogation of the tithe. The only time He expressed Himself on the tithe He gave His approval of it:

> "How terrible of you teachers of the Law and Pharisees! Impostors! You give to God one tenth even of the seasoning herbs, such as mint, dill, and cummin, but you neglect to obey the really important teachings of the Law, such as justice and mercy and honesty. These you should practice without neglecting the others."[4]

While rebuking His severest critics, Jesus admits that in tithing they were doing what should not be neglected. He rebukes them for omitting the "weightier matters of the law" but in the same breath rebukes the Christian who neglects tithing. The nontither comes just as surely under the rebuke of the Lord for leaving the tithe unpaid as did the Jew for not doing the "weightier matters."

In considering Jesus and the tithe, we should not overlook the significant statement in Matthew 22:21. The Pharisees had confronted Jesus in regard to paying taxes to

Caesar. Jesus asked whose image and superscription the coin bore. They answered, "Caesar's." "All right," Jesus replied, "Render to Caesar what is his, and to God what is His."

Jesus, no doubt, meant to say that Caesar had a right to the tax, and He was thus understood. But what are the things that belong to God? With the Jewish background the answer no doubt would be "the tithes." Early Christians paid the tax to Caesar and the tithes to God through the church. The least that the statement of Jesus could have meant was, "Render to Caesar the tax, and to God the tithe."

There can be little doubt that Jesus Himself paid the tithe. From the age of twenty to thirty He worked at the carpenter trade and earned money subject to the tithe. While there is no direct statement that Jesus paid the tithe, or that He did not pay it, we should note the following:

1. Tithing was a well-established principle among the Jews. Every devout Jew tithed. Jesus was brought up under Jewish training.

2. Jesus said that He came to fulfill the law. Is it not reasonable to believe that He fulfilled the law of the tithe also?

3. The Pharisees tried in every way to accuse Jesus, yet they never charged Him of violating the principle of the tithe. Had He not tithed, He most certainly would have been challenged by the Pharisees.

4. Jesus' standard was always higher than the law, never lower. Matthew 5:17-48.

5. Jesus' example in other things would lead one to believe He was faithful in paying tithes. He was circumcised the eighth day according to the law. He was presented at the Temple in the rite of redemption as a firstborn son. Luke 2:22, 23. He was taken to the feasts at Jerusa-

lem where the tithe or its equivalent was spent. Later He attended these feasts with His disciples. He deemed it in order to be baptized "to fulfill all righteousness." He instructed the lepers to show themselves to the priests according to the law of Moses. When we notice His perfect record in keeping the law, we must believe that He did not omit anything as important or universal as the tithe.

Jesus took both the Sabbath and the tithe for granted. While He did not command either, He certainly advocated both by precept and example. Jesus not only endorsed the tithe but went beyond the tithe in His endorsement. The widow who threw into the treasury all that she had was commended by Jesus. Jesus asked the rich young ruler to sell all and give to the poor. He seemingly approved the practice of Zacchaeus in giving half of his goods to feed the poor. He declared that the disciples would be rewarded for forsaking all.

According to Jesus the tithe, as well as justice, mercy, and faith were "matters of the law." Tithes were not types like sacrifices and the Sabbath which were fulfilled and replaced by something better, nor, like circumcision, was it declared unnecessary. The only valid argument against the tithe for the Christian is the argument "beyond the tithe."

Tithes and the Post-Apostolic Church

Many of the early church fathers have expressed themselves with regard to the tithe. They leave no question as to whether or not the Christian should pay the tithe. Many of these fathers were themselves won from paganism. We will notice the testimony of a few of them.[5]

Irenaeus (AD 120-202) declares, "The precepts of the perfect life are the same in each testament. . . . The Lord did not abrogate the law which also those who are justified

189

by faith did observe, previous to the giving of the law, but extended them."

Origen (185-253): "It is fit and profitable that the first-fruits be offered unto the priests of the gospel also, for so also hath the Lord ordained, that they who preach the gospel should live of the gospel."

Cyprian (200-258): "The tribe of Levi had no inheritance, but was supported by tithes, that they might devote themselves entirely to divine service. . . . Which reasoning and form is now held in matters affecting the clergy, that those who are promoted to clerical ordination in the Lord's church should on no account be called away from these divine duties . . . but . . . receiving from the altar, as it were, tithes from the fruit of the earth."

Ambrose (340-397): "It is not enough to bear the name if we do not the works of Christians; and the Lord hath commanded that the tithe of all our fruits, cattle, etc., be annually required. . . . The nine parts are given to you; but if you will not give tithes, you shall be reduced to a tenth."

Augustine (354-430): "By the grace of Christ (dearest brethren) the day is now at hand, in which we ought to gather the harvest, and therefore should be thinking about returning thanks to God who gave it, both in the matter of making offerings and rendering tithes. For God who has designed to give the whole has condescended to seek back from us the tithe, doubtless for our profit, not His own."

Augustine (354-430) brings to a close a sermon on Malachi 3:10 by saying, "For tithes are required as a matter of debt, and who has been unwilling to give them has been guilty of robbery."

Chrysostom (347-407): "How great a disgrace is this, that what among the Jews was no matter of astonishment or celebrity, has now among Christians become a matter

190

of surprise. If it were a dangerous thing to fail in paying tithes then, to be sure, it is a much more dangerous thing now."

Innocent III said, "God has commanded the payment of tithes to Himself as a token of His universal ownership."

In the Constitutions of the Holy Apostles,[6] believed to have been written the last of the third century, we read:

"All the first fruits of the winepress, the threshing floor, the oxen and the sheep, shalt thou give the priests, that thy storehouses and garners and the other products of thy land may be blessed, and thou mayest be strengthened with corn and wine and oil, and the herds of thy cattle and flocks of thy sheep may be increased. Thou shalt give a tenth of thy increase to the poor and to the stranger. All the first fruits of thy hot bread, of thy barrels of wine, or oil, or honey, or grapes, or the first fruits of other things, shalt thou give to the priests; but those of silver and garments, and all sorts of possessions, to the orphans and to the widow."

Many more quotations could be made from the writings of early Christians. Along many lines their writings are more or less obscure, but on the matter of the tithe their voices ring clear and emphatic. Ten of the early Councils, up to the year 790, ordered all Christians to tithe.

The Council of Seville, 590: "Let every husbandman and every artisan make a just tithing of his business. For as the Lord hath given everything, so from everything He demands the tithe, whether from fruit or field."

The Council of Macon, 585: "The divine laws also taking care of the ministers of the church that they might have their hereditary portion, have commanded all people to pay the tithe, that the clergy being hindered by no sort of employment, may be at leisure for spiritual duty of their ministry. Which laws the whole body of Christians for a long time kept inviolate, but now by degrees, almost all of them have shown themselves prevaricators of those laws since they neglect to fulfill the things which have been divinely ordained."

A later council, the Council of Trent, 1550, took the following action: "The payment of tithes is due to God, and they who refuse to pay them or hinder those who give them usurp the property of another. Wherefore the Holy Synod enjoins on all, of whatsoever rank or condition they be, that they henceforth pay in full the tithes to which they are bound in the law of the church and they who withhold or hinder them shall be excommunicated, nor shall they be absolved from the crime until full restitution has been made."

Charlemagne commanded tithes to be collected within all the portions of the Holy Roman Empire over which he ruled for the support of the church. The tithe was first enjoined in England in 786, in Germany and France in the ninth century, and in Scandinavian countries in the eleventh century. Difficulty in collecting the tithes led to their abandonment in most countries except England. Henry VII relieved the owners of great estates of the duty.[7] In England the tithe was considered as one of the inviolable rights of the church.

Dangers to Be Avoided in Teaching Tithing

Advocates of tithing are well aware that there are dangers to be avoided in teaching and promoting tithing. These dangers, however, are not inherent in tithing itself, but as real as in any standard of Christianity. The difficulty is not with the law but with the approach. Whenever standards become ends in themselves and become more important than persons or than the cause of Christ, they become legalistic and dangerous. There is the danger of self-righteousness or pharisaism. Like the Pharisee, we may thank God that we are better than others. Self-righteousness makes for an empty religion today just as it did in Jesus' day.

The danger of legalism is a real danger. It is my conviction, however, that most Christians who are tithing today are not motivated by legalism, but by grace. They are responding out of hearts of love to the grace of God. It should be said, however, that criticism of Old Testament legalism, motivated by a desire to escape generous giving is also unworthy of a Christian. One dominated by the spirit of materialism may stand in need of a "schoolmaster."

There is also a danger of making tithing a substitute for stewardship. One may make it the ceiling of giving, or he may feel that because he has given the tithe neither God nor the church has further claim on his life and talents. He may take the "hands-off" attitude toward the nine tenths. A steward must realize that he is steward of the full ten tenths, and that his life, time, and talents also come under the lordship of Christ.

There is also the danger of overemphasizing the "give-to-get" motive. To some opponents of tithing this is a real stumbling block. Yet this motive is held up time and again by the Almighty (Prov. 3:9, 10; 11:24, 25; Mal. 3:10; Mt. 6:33; 2 Cor. 9:6). What do these passages mean? Is not God interested in this area of our lives? To prosper is a legitimate desire, but it must not become a primary motive. Tithing should never be held up as a guarantee to prosperity or as something magic. But the Christian may always expect the blessings God promises for faithfulness.

In general, the proponents of tithing recognize these dangers and warn against them. They know, however, that these errors are not inherent in tithing, but are just as real dangers in other Christian standards. One may become legalistic about baptism, pharisaical about church attendance. He may make church membership a substitute for Christian experience or belong to a certain denomination for financial gain. He may live a good moral life for any of the above motives. What shall we do about this? Shall we teach against morality, church membership, and Christian ordinances? Certainly not. We teach against and try to avoid the errors, but keep on practicing what is right.

Advantages in the Practice of Tithing

Proponents of tithing recognize a number of distinct advantages in accepting the tithe as a standard of giving. In the first place, it has a biblical basis. Tithing was a law of the Hebrew society. It was widely practiced by the Jews of Jesus' day. Our Lord Himself said it was something that should not be left undone. The Apostle Paul advocates proportionate giving, giving according to God's gifts to us. In the Old Testament giving as God prospered meant rendering tithes. With Paul it certainly would not have meant less.

The tithe is a starting point within the reach of all. If the income is small, the amount given will not be large. On the other hand, to whom more is given, more is required. If one does not start tithing on small amounts, he often will not begin at all. John D. Rockefeller, Sr., was asked if he tithed. His answer was, "Yes, I tithe. My first wages amounted to around $1.50 a week. The first week I took the $1.50 home to my mother and she held the money in her lap and explained to me that she would be happy if I would give a tenth of it to the Lord. I did and from that week to this day I have tithed every dollar that God has entrusted to me, and I want to say to you that if I had not tithed the first dollar I made, I would not have tithed the first million dollars I made."

Tithing stewardship starts the believer in a challenging course of partnership with God in material things. This will help purify his heart and mind of selfish things. Generous and proportionate giving is a good antidote against the cancer of covetousness. This consciousness of partnership with God through stewardship will increase one's interest in the church of Christ and in His kingdom. An inevitable result of pledging a significant portion of one's income to the church wll be an increase of interest in what the church is doing. One's interest will follow the generous gift, sacrificially given to Christ and His church.

Christian tithing helps put God first in money matters. God's people in Old Testament times were asked to put God first by offering Him the firstfruits of their fields and vineyards and the firstlings of the flocks and herds. There can be little doubt that setting aside a tenth of one's income for the purposes of God would contribute significantly to giving God His rightful place in our lives. Israel was asked to keep the Sabbath that they might know that God was Lord (Ex. 31:13). They were asked to tithe all the increase that they might learn to fear the Lord always (Deut. 14:23). Setting aside one day in seven and one dollar out of ten for the praise of God's glorious grace can do much for a meaningful relationship between man and his God.

The tithe plan is effective. Churches that have successfully promoted tithing stewardship rank at the top in per capita giving. On the other hand often pastors who oppose the teaching and practice of tithing are pastoring churches that fall shamefully below the tithe of the Old Testament, and far below the average for the denomination. Many churches that were struggling with a debt and with inadequate funds quickly solved their financial problem with a tithing program. If all Christians would tithe their income

195

to the Lord, it would eliminate empty church treasuries, mission books in the red, curtailed mission programs, and church institutions begging for funds.

Worldly · methods of fund raising — bazaars, raffles, lottery, and bingo — could forever be discarded if churches would promote scriptural tithing.

The following statement from *Reader's Digest* might give an idea what the tithe could do:

"If every church member in the U.S. was suddenly bereft of all income and assets and placed on public relief, and then tithed this meager sum, the income of American churches, under those circumstances, would be about 35 percent greater than it is now."

The tithe is definite and concrete. It helps avoid the danger of giving everything in general but nothing in particular. The nontither stands in danger of saying "all I have is God's" and ending up giving a mere pittance to the Lord and His church whom he claims to love and serve. Unless one has a systematic plan of giving there is a danger of meeting all other needs and wants first and having little left to give. When one sets aside a tithe and dedicates it to the Lord he can be more objective in his giving. When a worthy cause is presented there is money that has been dedicated and one does not have to weigh the cause against personal needs and wants. The cause presented is weighed only against other worthy causes.

The practice of tithing will help Christians to give heroically and sacrificially. At the beginning most people will feel that they can hardly afford to tithe. After one begins tithing other sacrifices will follow. Many who begin with ten percent go on to fifteen, twenty, and beyond. William Colgate began with the tithe when receiving a small wage. He kept increasing the amount until he was giving all his income for the work of the Lord. This likely would never have happened had he not been pointed to tithing stewardship.

Tithing has been a source of blessing to thousands of faithful Christians. They have testified of untold joy that came to them through partnership with God through the tithing-covenant. The blessings were both spiritual and temporal. These people would not want to return to their former haphazard way of giving to the Lord's work. Not only has it been a blessing to individuals but to churches as well. Tithing churches have experienced revival and spiritual renewal through fellowship with Christ in the stewardship of giving.

During the past years I have given a series of stewardship messages in over 250 churches in the United States and Canada. Many are the testimonies I have received from cheerful givers. I want to give one that I received in a church in Illinois. While waiting to deliver the last message of the series an usher came down the aisle and handed me a note. It read as follows:

Dear Brother Kauffman,

I am a working person getting a weekly check that isn't any more than enough to take care of our expenses. After hearing you preach on tithing my wife and I knelt down on our knees and promised God we would by faith take ten percent of my next check and give it to the Lord. We knew at the time it was impossible to make our check reach, but we said we would just wait and see how the Lord can work it out. Just two days later my boss said to me, "I'm going to give you a chance to make more money." Now he knew nothing about our decision on tithing just two days before. It is now possible to earn far more than the tithe I will take from my check. I am thrilled to see it work so soon. I'm in your audience tonight and am certainly glad for this teaching.

197

I am aware that the second to the last sentence will make some people unhappy. They will say that neither God nor the tithe works that way. Who says they do not? While we should not promise people it will always happen that way, hundreds of Christians have experienced that it does happen. Will not faith in God's Word make us believe this does happen?

Paul told the Corinthians that if they sowed bountifully they would reap bountifully. God said, "Bring the tithes and see if you won't be blessed." Why do we object and why are we so afraid to teach the Bible truth about God rewarding the faithful giver? God is a rewarder of those who diligently seek Him and hundreds of faithful Christians are diligently seeking His will in presenting tithes and offerings. They are finding that God is a rewarder. When we fail to preach blessing and reward for obedience to God we are not preaching the full gospel.

Oral Roberts teaches a truth which I believe more of us should emphasize. He urges people to sow "faith seed" by giving a generous gift. Then he says, "Expect a miracle." Too few people really expect a miracle; really believe that God is a rewarder. It is neither wrong to want nor to expect a reward for faithfulness. In fact, we dishonor God if we do not; we don't believe His promises; we belie His true nature. It seems a bit strange that some people are so opposed to teaching rewards for tithing, then spend most of their lives trying to get rewards in other ways.

The Christian will have an open hand to receive and a ready hand to give. His primary purpose in tithing is not financial gain or blessing, but as a steward his receiving hand must be open to receive God's gifts.

Recently I heard a man who had practiced tithing for decades tell of some of the rewards he had experienced.

He said no one could tell him that he had less today than he would have had he not tithed. It was a satisfaction to know that he had carried his share of the church and mission load. It was a pleasure to have something to give when a needy cause arose. He did not have to argue with himself whether he could afford to give; the money had been dedicated previously. It made giving a pleasure. He has for a number of years been giving considerably above the tithe. For him tithing has been a joyous and exciting partnership with God.

Another advantage many tithers mention is that it helps them to be better stewards of the nine tenths. This often accounts for the reason why some people make ends meet better after adopting the tithing plan. A businessman gives the following testimony:

"In the last twenty years I have spoken on tithing to thousands of church members and I have yet to meet one who faithfully tithed his income without receiving a real blessing. In most cases the tither's income increases, but where it does not, the universal experience seems to be that the Lord makes the nine tenths go further than the ten tenths did before."

"Tithing helps us to remember that all belongs to God and serves to make us more economical and systematic in our use of money."

In her book, *Spending for Happiness,* Elsie Stapleton reports that she has helped prepare thousands of family budgets and says:

"I have worked out more than two hundred budgets for the group known as tithers. These are the good souls who give 10 percent of their income to the kingdom causes. Never have I known a tither to be in the red. Their spending patterns could well be models for other

199

incomes in comparable brackets. You may wonder why the members of such a financially stable and well-integrated group would be interested in seeking professional guidance for their budgets. I do not know whether it is true of all tithers, but it was the case with everyone who consulted me about a spending plan — each one wanted to be absolutely certain that he was spending 90 percent of his money as wisely as possible. But the 10 percent set aside for tithing — that was untouchable.

"I was interested enough, at one time, to gather together all the tithing budgets I had worked out. They were indeed, fine spending patterns. Intuitively or consciously, the spenders had allocated their money in well-balanced outlays. As I remember them, they were all singularly well adjusted, financially and spiritually. Excellent business people too. They knew the value of money and they spent their earnings on what was most important to them. The 10 percent was the most vital of their outlays."

What if I Decide to Give Less Than the Tithe?

If as Christians we are faithfully seeking to be loyal to Christ, but decide on a standard lower than the tithe, we must believe the following:

1. Jesus, our Lord, sets a lower standard than did Moses under the law.

2. The gospel of Jesus Christ sounds a retreat.

3. The Christian under grace has less obligation to God and his fellowmen than did the Jews under the law.

4. The stern demands of the law produce better results than the gospel of grace. Sinai is stronger than Calvary.

5. Either Christ's cause is less worthy than Judaism or needs less to carry it on.

6. That Christians receive less from God than did the Jew and therefore not as much is required of them.

7. That Christians are not as able to give as were the Jews.

Any thoughtful Christian knows that all of these are false. Every reason that existed in the Hebrew society for giving tithes exists now. The blessings of God and His unmerited gifts are more abundantly given to Christians today. The need today is as urgent as it ever was and never was the obligation to the unsaved greater than today. Every argument for the tithe which could be brought to bear on the Jew applies with increased emphasis today. Any argument against the tithe should never justify less than the tithe.

Giving Above the Tithe

It would seem that the only argument against the tithe by affluent Christians would be that the tithe is too little for most Christians. There are many who sincerely feel that way. A. A. Hyde of Mentholatum fame held that the tithe was for the poor and those of moderate circumstances. Those in comfortable circumstances should by all means give above the tithe.

In the *Gospel Herald,* August 29, 1972, Ronald J. Sider gave some provocative and, I think, sensible suggestions. The article is entitled "The Graduated Tithe." He speaks of the poverty in the world and the affluence of American Christians and the tendency to splurge in unnecessary luxury. He suggests that some dramatic move is necessary to save us from creeping materialism and suggests a way to break the materialistic stranglehold.

His plan is that the family sit down and carefully consider what it would take to live in reasonable comfort, but without some of the luxuries. If the figure we come up with is $7,500, we give to the church 10 percent of that amount. On each additional $1,000 our giving would be increased by five percent on that $1,000 as shown by the following table.

201

Income	Percent Given to Church	Amount to Lord's Work
First $7,500	10	$750
Next 1,000	15	150
Next 1,000	20	200
Next 1,000	25	250
Next 1,000	30	300
Next 1,000	35	350
Total $12,500		$2,000

This method of giving should appeal to many Christians in our affluent society who have escaped the ensnarement of materialism and covetousness, or wish to escape it.

Another Example of Graduated Giving

Years ago a prosperous Christian businessman was asked about his method of giving. He answered, "In consecrating my life anew to God, aware of the ensnaring influence of riches and the necessity of deciding on a plan of charity before wealth should bias my judgment, I adopted the following system." In brief, his plan was to give 10 percent of net profits until the profits reached $500 per month. When his income exceeded that amount he would give 12 1/2 percent on the entire net profits. When net profits exceeded $700 per month he would give 15 percent of net profits. With every increase of $200 in profits the percent given was increased 2 1/2 percent so that at $1,500 profit per month the giving was 25 percent. After acquiring a certain amount of capital, giving was increased to 50 percent, and when capital had increased to where he felt it was sufficient to run his business he gave all his net profits.

He gives his testimony, "It is now several years since I adopted this plan and under it I have built up a handsome capital and have been prospered beyond my most sanguine expectations. Although constantly giving, I have never yet reached the bottom of my fund. This system has been of great advantage to me, enabling me to feel that my life is directly employed for God." [9]

This worthy example of giving according to God's gifts to us most certainly indicates faithful and responsible Christian stewardship. This method surely should remove any criticism of tithing, even though it did begin with tithing.

A Quote Worthy of Notice

"One of the things that bothers me when tithing is under discussion is for people to spend their time framing up objections to it. I have heard it called hard and legalistic. It can be termed unfair because 10 percent of $3,000 income is really a greater sacrifice than 10 percent of $10,000 income. It can be said that there are weightier matters for the Christian life. It can be said that some people give a great deal of time and therefore ought not be expected to give as much money as others. And so on. These objections disturb me because they seem usually to be defense mechanisms triggered in minds already determined to excuse themselves for not giving 10 percent. They are heard more frequently from those with good incomes than from those with poor incomes. The only answer I can give is that once one tries tithing they seem to be irrelevant."

He further states that many get more joy and satisfaction out of the 90 percent when they practice tithing. Generosity brings joy, and usually people who give 10 percent are better managers of the 90 percent than they were of the 100 percent before tithing. [10]

The Author's Personal Testimony

Few practices have brought greater satisfaction and

reward to me than the practice of proportionate giving of my income. As a youth I felt the need of training for Christian service and enrolled in a Christian institution. I had scarcely half enough resources to pay for the first year but trusted God to see me through. At the close of the year, with a college debt, I went to work to pay off the debt and lay up for the second year. In the meantime, I heard some scriptural teaching on Christian tithing. I was convinced it was a practice I should adopt. But a voice seemed to say, "Not you, you are giving everything to prepare yourself for Christian service. If you tithe you won't have enough for your education." Thank God I did not heed that voice. I knew I was dependent on God anyway and would do what I believed He was asking me to do.

At the close of the second year I was convinced that I was better off than I would have been had I not honored God with the tithe. I worked my way through college and came out without a debt. Since then while supporting a good-sized family and giving a great deal of time to the work of the church, there have been times when it was difficult to make ends meet, but I have endeavored to render to God what was His. I must testify to the goodness of God in supplying every need. Rather than being a hardship, tithing has brought joy and blessing. No one can make me believe it did not bring temporal blessing as well as spiritual blessings. God has prospered so that I can now know the joy of giving beyond the tithe.

Charles Cowman, missionary to Japan, began tithing a year after his conversion and later gave all his income to the Lord which was not absolutely needed for personal needs. He helped form a "Tithers League" in the Grace M.E. Church in Chicago that made worldly methods of fund raising unnecessary and that brought spiritual life and revival to the church. He said that the man who begins to tithe will have six genuine surprises. He will be surprised at:

1. The amount of money he has for the Lord's work;
2. The deepening of his own spiritual life in paying the tithe;
3. The ease in meeting his own obligations with nine tenths and with God's blessing;
4. The ease in going on from one tenth to larger giving;
5. The preparation this gives to be a faithful and wise steward over the nine tenths that remain;
6. Himself in not adopting the biblical plan sooner.[11]

Cowman recommended tithing for those whose faith is not strong enough for unconditional surrender but who are willing to accept God's challenge for a year and prayerfully observe His leading. He believed that seldom do any such recede from the covenant.

A noted Baptist minister raised the question, "How do we lay up treasures in heaven?" His answer was that only what is laid down here for Him will be laid up there. If you lay down a tenth for the Lord it is laid up there. If you use the nine tenths selfishly they will not be laid up there. But if you lay down the whole ten tenths in purpose, keeping it subject to the Lord, giving a tenth for the immediate purposes of God, and holding the nine tenths as a working capital and yet subject to His will, you lay it all up.[12]

> "What I spent, I had;
> What I kept, I lost;
> What I gave, I have."
> — An inscription from a tombstone

In Conclusion

"The tithe may be a fumbling standard of a person's

giving, and measured by the New Testament concept of grace, it is a poor place to stop, but for millions of Christians the tithe is a first and essential step in moving away from the kind of life which is dominated by materialistic desires. The tithe is a doorway to an abundant life.

"Tithing is an affirmation of faith in God. It is a recognition of His goodness. Because of human frailties, tithing may sometimes become legalistic or may lead to self-righteousness, but its basic principles are worship and surrender. Occasional misuse, caused by weakness, should not bar the Christian from the joy and satisfaction which come when, through the tithe, they acknowledge each one of God's mercies."[13]

"Tithing is a plan of God for growing Christians. The primary purpose of tithing is not to raise money but to build character. Tithing is God's plan for developing better men and women. Only when we recognize our stewardship to Him do we grow spiritually.

"The significance of the tithe is not money but men. Tithing acknowledges God as Owner. . . . Tithing teaches us to put God first."[14]

13

EXAMPLES
AND TESTIMONIES

"We want you to know, brothers, what God's grace has done in the churches in Macedonia. They have been severely tested by the troubles they went through; but their joy was so great that they were extremely generous in their giving, even though they were very poor" (2 Cor. 8:1, 2, TEV).

Many are the examples of faithful stewards and numerous the testimonies of joy that come from the lips of generous, faithful stewards. The following are given with the prayer that they may be seed falling on well-prepared soil, which will sprout, grow, and bear fruit in the lives of many.

1. A Brethren in Christ family is contributing a large amount each month to an inner-city program run by black evangelists. Whereas a year ago this important work was in danger of having to close for lack of funds, it is now on its feet.

2. A mission executive reports: "When I was in Argentina, I met a member of the church at Santa Rosa who challenged me with her dedication. After experiencing God's grace in her life, she told her pastor that she wanted

to give significantly to help build the church. She had no money, but asked her husband if she might put her engagement ring in the offering. Although he was not an evangelical Christian he agreed, and she gave the $300 ring one Sunday morning. I was able to hear her radiant testimony and see her joy in Christ."

3. Before the meeting of an annual session of the Southern Baptist Convention a generous man said to his pastor, "I have rented an entire floor of our best hotel for the week of the Convention. I want you to fill it with your friends."

4. The noted founder of the Moravians, Count Zinzendorf, disposed of his entire fortune, including honors and titles, saying, "Lord, I surrender all." He declared, "I have but one passion — it is He, it is He alone. The world is the field, and the field is the world: and henceforth that country shall be my home where I can be most used in winning souls to Christ."

5. John Ruskin gave himself and his money to God and humanity. At first he gave a tenth, then a third, then one half, and finally he gave all.

6. A man of Troy, New York, Harvey S. McLeod, after his conversion asked his pastor how he could make the most of himself. "Tithe," said the pastor. McLeod did so and helped many young men get an education and led hundreds to be tithers.

7. James L. Kraft of cheese fame said he had reached the verge of bankruptcy when he realized he had left God out of his business. He repented, made God his partner, and began tithing his income. Things rapidly improved for him and he became the world's largest cheese man. He zealously went about urging others to take God as partner, and do business for Him.

8. A man ninety years old, residing in a nursing

home, makes toy windmills attractively painted. He stands by the hour on main street with his mills and makes occasional sales. He recently wrote a Christian college, "Often my prayers are for your needs. I have no bank account. God gets one third of my windmills."

9. Brother Michael was a real estate broker in California and acquired a fortune exceeding $400,000. He considered himself a Christian but gave only enough to salve his conscience. He never read the Bible.

A few years ago he accepted Christ and became a real Christian. He now knows that Christ lives and that His teachings are in the Bible. His life was changed and he longed to serve Christ. He found "truck loads" of joy in giving. Concentrating on the Watts area, he sought to show the love of Christ in deeds as well as words. He has given away over a million Bibles, New Testaments, and Scripture portions. He loads his truck with food, fruit, clothing, and toys and gives it to the needy.

He has used up nearly all his fortune. His face radiated happiness as he told the reporter, "Finally I reached my objective of having it all working for the Lord." He is living now "as the Lord provides," and gets more joy out of life than when he owned a fortune of $400,000.[1]

10. A college freshman, whose parents are missionaries, recently sent a check to the Mission Board. It was a tithe of money she had earned for college expenses. She is convinced that as she honors God with her tithe, He will supply her needs.

11. The late A. A. Hyde, wealthy Mentholatum man of Wichita, Kansas, in writing to members of the family said, "I am frequently asked if I believe in tithing. I certainly do, though I was never a tither myself." After making a study of giving he felt that Christ's teaching in Matthew 6 ruled him out of the tithing class. The Sermon on the

Mount indicated to him that the tithe was for those without accumulated wealth. Persons with surplus means for outside investment were to "lay up" these treasures in heaven that their hearts may be there also. He believed that surplus wealth above one's own economic requirements should be used to relieve distress and promote truth and righteousness. He stated, "Increasingly in my later years has the great joy of giving to meet human needs and for world betterment come to me. The Lord grant that this joy and peace may come to each of you and to your descendants after you." [2]

12. A lumberman had tithed for many years and God prospered him. He increased God's part to 15 percent, then to 20 percent, and God continued to prosper him. Finally he bought a big planing mill and showed his gratitude by dedicating 50 percent of the profits to God's work. In later years more than $100,000 of profits were used to advance the kingdom.

13. When Spurgeon was only a boy he adopted the principle of giving a tenth to the Lord. Having won money as a prize for an essay on a religious subject, he felt he could not give less than one fifth of it. Afterward he was never able to deny himself the pleasure of giving a fifth; and, as everyone knows, God wonderfully blessed him and increased his means and his enjoyment of the luxury of giving. His was a case of lifelong proportionate, ungrudging giving. [3]

14. An automobile dealer testified, "I have learned that by forming a partnership with Christ and paying more attention to spiritual things and less to material things everything works out much better. I am much better off financially than I was before I started tithing but even if I had less money I would continue to tithe, for it has been the source of my happiest Christian experience. I have

learned that being a partner with Christ and having the privilege of handling a small portion of His business is worth more than all the world has to offer."

15. A banker with a fabulous salary gave up his job during World War I to give his services to his country. He said, "This is the time to cut expenses to the bone. Young men who spend money for flowers, candy, theatres and other luxuries for their girls; people who give rich dinners and decorate their homes lavishly for entertainments; all who buy things today that they can do without, are allies of the Kaiser."

Whose allies are we Christians if we spend large amounts of money lavishly and selfishly on ourselves when millions are in poverty and the needs of the kingdom are so urgent?

16. J. A. Schowalter, a farmer, businessman, and state legislator of Newton, Kansas, died in 1953. Through hard work and frugal living he accumulated a considerable estate of thousands of acres in Kansas and Oklahoma. He had intended to establish a foundation to perpetuate some of his concerns, primarily that of peace and peace education, aid to missionaries and ministers, resettlement of refugees, and promotion of brotherhood. He could not accomplish this before his death, but made provision for it in his last will and testament.

Shortly after his death the foundation was set up with assets slightly above one million dollars. Since that time more than a million dollars of income has been dispersed by the trustees of the foundation for overseas aid, physical and mental health, Christian worker retirement and preparation, international education, peace education, various studies and seminars, interracial programs, etc.

The income for distribution has been increasing steadily, and the original estate has increased considerably in value.

17. Four Christian business and professional men recently donated to a Christian college a restaurant valued at $200,000. The restaurant continues to pay taxes and is operated for the college by a separate corporation. This provides job openings for a number of students needing employment. There are plans to have the restaurant serve as a laboratory for training students in food services and food preparation. It now appears that this also will provide supplementary funds for the college.

18. Henry Thorton heard an appeal for missions and made out a check for five pounds. Before the ink was dry he was handed a telegram. As he read it he turned pale. He said to the visitor, "I have just received bad news. I have lost thousands of pounds. Give me back the check." The visitor expected the check would be canceled. Instead, Mr. Thorton made the check for 50 pounds saying, "God has just taught me that I may not have my property much longer, and that I must use it well."

19. A church in Ohio with a membership of only 103 helps support 72 missionaries in 22 different countries and in 19 states with an annual budget of $47,000. Pledges from this year's missionary conference reached a total of $64,000. Fifteen percent of the membership of the church are missionaries. The pastor manages a country general store during the week, but the weekends find him preaching two or three times, either in the home church or in neighboring churches. What would happen if all our churches would do as well?

20. Two Christians, one a lawyer and the other a businessman, were visiting Korea. They had as their guide and interpreter a missionary. As they were driving along they saw by the side of the road a young man pulling a crude plow and an old man holding the handles. "Stop," said the lawyer, "I want a picture of that." One of them

remarked to the missionary, "Those men must be very poor." The missionary informed them that these men had owned an ox but when money was needed for the church, they sold the ox and gave the money for the new church saying, "We can plow our land by hand." After a period of silence one of the men said, "That must have been a real sacrifice." "They did not consider it a sacrifice," said the missionary, "they were glad they had the ox to sell so they could help with the church."

After they returned from the tour, the lawyer showed the picture to his pastor, telling him the story. Then he said, "Pastor, I want you to double the amount of my pledge to the church, and please give me some 'plow work.' I have never really made a sacrifice."

21. An article appeared in the *Wichita Eagle,* entitled "Tithing Practice Convinced Bank." The writer stated that he had begun a promising business some years ago. One day the banker called and asked that he come to the bank with his records to explain a large overdraft. He showed the banker the records and informed him that income was on the way. He was asked to explain an expense item. He explained it was his tithe, that he practiced giving a tenth of his income. The banker said that was commendable but that he had better wait until he was able to afford it. He replied, "If you wait until you can afford to tithe, you'll never do it. That is one expense that stands. I won't cut back there under any circumstances."

The next morning the banker called him and said, "We decided to cover your deficit . . . and in order to give you a little breathing room, we will extend your credit limit up to $25,000." The banker stated that the men at the bank were impressed with his habit of tithing his income and "we decided that anyone with that kind of conviction was a good risk." [4]

Testimonies

The testimonies given here are those received in response to stewardship messages given by the author.

"Once more I have been made to realize my own failure in this area and have renewed my pledge of stewardship. I have decided that a few items of clothing I had anticipated buying in the near future are unnecessary. Truly the tithe I give back to the Lord is just a beginning, and I know I'm not yet really giving." — *Pennsylvania.*

o   o   o

"After hearing some of your lectures on 'Stewardship' we have willed our home to our home church." — *Tennessee.*

o   o   o

"We thank you; we thank you very much for ministering God's Word to us so plainly and forcefully. . . .

"We have been married 16 years. In the second or third year we came across a little brown book on tithing. Ever since then we tithed, not the net income, but every dollar that passed through our hands. Ever since then we prospered greatly materially. . . .

"But the greatest blessing in tithing is the inward joy it brings. We would never, never want to go back to the old way of giving at random to the Lord. Of course, very often the tithe is not enough to meet God's requests on our purse. Then He supplied every time, the necessary funds to fulfill the obligation as we felt it.

"During the duration of World War II I was allowed to stay at home, being the only man on the farm, but had to pay $15.00 monthly as a C.O. to the Red Cross. It came to me in church on Friday that what had to be always available for our earthly government during wartime, should I not joyfully and gratefully offer that to my Savior's work in peacetime? And so I would like to offer the monthly

$15 from now on to the Prince of Peace." — *Canada*.

o   o   o

"I did so much appreciate the messages that you gave us. I praise God for an awakening in our church on the subject. . . . Already many of my friends are giving systematically. In our church in Puerto Rico tithing was taught as one of the doctrines of the church. Our people there, poor as they are, bring their tithes to church every Sunday." — *Indiana*.

Testimonies from Today's Stewards

To secure the testimonies of some leading churchmen of today a number of pastors, church leaders, and Christian laymen were invited to send in their testimonies on stewardship. May God use these to challenge others to joyful giving and service.

A Church Leader

"In our first pastorate we received an offering once a month which averaged less than $200. And we gave full time to the ministry. Early the Lord led us to give generously and we found that the blessings of giving are not material but especially spiritual. We saw our congregation grow and the giving triple in four years.

"After several years in the ministry we had a 14-year-old car and a growing family. Putting a few dollars in savings each month we finally saved $300.

"Then a special mission need arose. The Lord seemed to say clearly in my study one morning that the $300 should be given. I shuddered at the idea and thought of many things we thought we needed as a family. We were already giving considerably above the tithe.

"Testing and sharing the idea with my wife, she

immediately said, 'Sure, let's give it. One never becomes poor from what he gives away.' We went to the bank and drew out the $300, the largest amount we had ever drawn out of any bank up to that time, even for college and seminary payments.

"Our needs have always been met. The Lord has taught us something of the contentment He speaks of 'If we have food and clothing, with these let us be content' (1 Tim. 6:9). A sincere effort at being a good steward helps one to live simply and takes away that craving for things which never satisfy.

"Over the years our income has risen. We are still in full-time church work. We have also sought to increase our giving each year, so that now we are able to give 30 percent and by doing so also solve the problem of war taxes. We rejoice many times for the privilege of giving. Many in our world cannot give because they have nothing."

A Pastor

"One night before we were married, my sweetheart stated that she was going to begin to tithe her income and I said, if you are going to do it, I will too. This was the beginning of our commitment to Christ in the area of Christian stewardship.

"After marriage we started farming for our means of livelihood. Although the income was not too great, this being soon after the depression, we did continue to tithe.

"Within a few years we felt led to commit ourselves to the support of a foreign missionary. At the time the support of a missionary was $600 per year, which to us seemed like a huge sum of money. There were times when we needed to borrow the money to meet our commitment, but God was always faithful in supplying our needs.

"Some years later God called us into the Christian

ministry in another state. After making this move we felt that we would need to discontinue our missionary support, as the amount was now over $1,000 per year. I wrote a letter to the Mission Board stating our intentions, but didn't send it right away. After praying some more about our decision, I said to my wife, 'I can't send the letter, let's just trust the Lord to supply the needed funds.' She agreed, so I tore up the letter and again God was faithful. The amount has now gone up to $2,000 a year and God has always supplied the needs.

"The tithe was just the beginning. Since then we have raised the percent of giving to 12 percent, then 15 percent, then 20 percent, and now 25 percent. When we made our commitment to support a missionary we were deeply in debt. God has blessed us during the years so that we are no longer in debt. The only way is to take God's portion out of each check first. Giving has been and is a great blessing to us.

"As a result of our taking Christian stewardship seriously in the area of giving, our children have also caught on. They started tithing of their income while they were in grade school, and have continued even while in college when they were working their way through school and their income was quite meager.

" 'It is more blessed to give than to receive' is certainly true."

A Christian Layman

"As my wife and I were contemplating marriage some twenty-five years ago, she said that there were two things that she desired to have established in our home to be. The first was family worship, the second was that we give a tithe of our income to the Lord. As a nominal Christian at that time, I was not too excited over either of them, but especially did I frown on the tithing, since I was teaching school at the time for a nominal sum of $2,400 per year.

"But I wanted the woman, so I consented. As the children came, grew, became involved, scattered, the family worship at times prospered, dwindled, rallied, and at intervals even came to temporary stops. But we never slipped in our tithing. We have always skimmed off the top 10 percent of our gross income and given it to the work of the church, the spreading of the gospel. I speak not as a Pharisee, but as one who is convinced that this is God's minimum plan for His children. What a blessing it has been! It has provided an effortless way for us to give to the church, to missions, to the building up of the kingdom of God.

"I have never, never regretted keeping our tithe book. It is a small account book in which we record that 10 percent of our income and the various agencies to which we then distribute it. It is the Lord's expense account. It is a thrill to look back over it, to recall the times and places where we felt the Holy Spirit directed us to minister through giving.

"My wife brought many beautiful things into our marriage. I consider her insistence that we tithe one of the greatest. I praise God that we have been blessed with the privilege of giving in such a manner for a quarter of a century."

Another Christian Layman

"I have particularly noticed how many people seem to waste both money and time. Since time wasted cannot be made up in any way, I have felt that wasting time is even worse than misspending money.

"Every person living in America should minimumly

tithe. It seems relatively easy in the United States to earn money.

"In money affairs, the government taxing authorities years ago allowed a 10 percent deduction on the tithe. Later they changed it to 30 percent, and within the last few years it has again been changed to 50 percent. Any Christian steward not going along with this in his own affairs, should certainly have an adequate personal Christian reason not to.

"Personally I believe that time spent in accumulating wealth, beyond the family's year to year needs, also wastes time. Even so, however, substantial estates often accumulate. The government takes a big bite out of these if they are not appropriately disposed of beforehand. Social security, medicare, plus what most institutions provide additionally today, provide adequately for old age and other contingencies. There should be no excuse for anyone having an estate to be settled or disposed of or divided. Normally all the children by that time have finished their education and have found their life calling and can easily be on their own.

"Today the church has multitudinous places in almost every part of the world where financial gifts can be productively used. May a larger and larger number of us see this today and so act."

A Christian Educator

"My wife and I and our children have tithed our incomes and have always tried to give above the minimum tithe. In years past, during depressions and a long succession of unusual medical expenses, this has not been easy. However, it has always been a blessing. Now that our children are grown we can give a much greater share. It is very gratifying to have money set aside and available and to look for worthy causes which should be supported rather than to feel that giving must be on the basis of requests and requirements."

A *Christian Ophthalmologist*

"It was my privilege to grow up in a Christian home where my parents taught and practiced the scriptural precept of tithing. It was only natural that when my dear wife and I established our home that we tried to accept and practice this also. But with the passing of time I began to question this precept. It was scriptural only in the light of the Old Testament but is not taught directly as such in the New Testament. And as I thought about it I began to see tithing as a guideline or a standard for giving; it became my conviction that giving a tenth could only be the minimum — there actually is no way you can give too much or outgive the Lord. That if given in good conscience and with a contrite heart, the more you give to God, the more He gives back to you.

"A few years later I was challenged to prepare a dissertation on Christian stewardship and found it expedient to restructure this concept all over again, but in greater depth than before. It became a real struggle for me as I tried to relate the meaning of stewardship within the context of New Testament teachings. However, all my struggling and searching culminated into a glorious and beautiful fulfillment of my efforts when I read the first seven verses of Acts chapter three where Peter and John went up to the temple to pray and met the lame man at the gate begging for alms. Peter looked on him and said, 'Silver and gold have I none; but *such as I have give I thee*.' This to me is the KEY which unlocks the doors for Christian stewardship.

"People who are in need and beg for their need are not asking just for a hand-out. Their need is not only for money; they want you to give part of yourself, your talents and abilities, 'such as you have.' And even those around you who may not be begging in any way will still respond to a warm smile, a friendly handshake, a pat on the back, a word of encouragement, a token which indicates that you care for them, time spent in the ministry of prayer. The list for giving 'such as you have' can become endless but so also are the rewards. And the giving of 'silver and gold' will become spontaneous and secondary when you share of yourself — giving away that which God has entrusted to you but cannot be bought."

A Missionary

"I have always believed in being a good steward of what the Lord has entrusted to my care, and I have always wanted to give my fair share. But it was a long time before I discovered the value of planned giving. Careful analysis showed me that haphazard and emotional giving did not total anything like a full tithe, even though I thought I was tithing.

"I now have a specific amount I put into the offering envelope each Sunday. When I am away from my home church for one or more Sundays I make up the full amount for the Sundays I missed. In this way I know exactly how much I give in the church offering in a year.

"But this is not all my giving. There are the schools and colleges, special offerings, Sunday school class, the United Fund, as well as other funds — all these tax-deductible. As a citizen and member of my community I am obliged to give to most or all of these. And, of course, there is the personal gift and charity giving that I may or may not keep books on. But keeping account is important or else I may be deceiving myself into thinking I am giving more than I am. I know a man who, in his old age, sent a thousand dollars to his mission board. This was, he said, to make up the full tithe just in case he made mistakes in his calculations over the years.

"There is joy and spiritual release in giving. Finally, the only truly Christian motivation for giving is to give because Christ gave His all for me."

A Church Leader

"As a boy growing up in a Western church, I heard and accepted teaching on tithing. Coming into earning, I practiced giving a tenth, not in a strict legalistic fashion, for I was not a good housekeeper. But conscientiously I gave at least a tenth.

"When I married, my wife had the same convictions. We found ways of keeping our living standard down so that we always could give the Lord His portion.

"As the years passed and our income went up, we increased the proportion of our giving to about one fifth. This has been the level of our giving for many years.

"After one of our changes of location it became clear that we could rent more cheaply than make monthly payments, pay taxes, and maintain a property. By not owning real estate we were able to give more.

"We have never had a large income and so have not handled much money. But the greatest financial pleasure we have ever had is giving money to the Lord through His church.

"Since the practice of church budgets has come in, we have welcomed the opportunity to make an estimate of our income so that we can know what our weekly offering should be. And we have always been happy when we could exceed this amount.

"Our practice of stewardship comes from our belief that we and all that we have belong to the Lord. It is a joy to express this concept in terms of financial outgo."

A Pastor

"This is my testimony. A testimony must be personal. Although I have had strong convictions regarding giving prior to 1942, it was in that year that I felt I ought to accept what I considered the biblical tithes and offerings teaching. The conviction hit me when the financial going was tough! Financial miracles did not occur.

"When I got married I discovered that my wife understood more fully what stewardship means. We graduated to her 15 percent offerings. Because of my wide experience I have had the opportunity to observe how 'the world' lives. Honesty prompted me to admit that Jesus Christ is more worthy than 'the world.' I also had to admit that seeking to live a solid Christian life meant great savings over against what others were doing.

"In my studies I discovered that the Bible nowhere teaches that the tithe means a flat 10 percent of our earnings. The Old Testament tithe system included far more than that. We moved to the 20 percent giving pattern.

"To give 20 percent one cannot live as others. For example one booklet on financial advice has the person spending so much money that finally only $100 is left for all medical, personal, and giving factors. In my judgment this is ridiculous even from a human standpoint.

"As we experienced the joy of giving we found we got more satisfaction out of this form of 'spending' than other ways of using money. Thus, giving 20 percent plus is not a minus, but a plus! Most of our giving goes through the two local churches with which we are associated. However, we also give to causes not represented by the churches. One of the greatest satisfactions in seeking to be honest with God with our money is that we can work so vitally toward issues and we can meet challenges — spread of the gospel, Bibles for the world, food for the hungry, etc.

"Giving as the Lord leads has its own reward. Not necessarily prosperity. Not ease. But Matthew 16:24 does not promise ease but it does lead to John 10:10."

Charles Cowman

In less than six months after Charles Cowman, an outstanding example of Christian stewardship, was soundly converted he had led over 70 of his fellow-workers to the Lord. He won them in odd moments at the office, and not on company time. A gracious revival was going on in the office without an outside evangelist.

Some months later he was attending a Christian convention and heard a message on tithing. The message was for him, and a year after his conversion he opened an account with the Lord. From each monthly check the tithe was set apart for the Lord's work. On the flyleaf of his account book was written, "The tithe is the Lord's," and "The connection between man's tithes and God's windows." From that day to the end of his life nothing came to his hands that was not tithed.

With tithing came a new concern for the use of the nine tenths. How large should the "offerings" be? In his account book he had a page marked "offerings." He was greatly blessed by his generous giving. His wife wrote, "It would be a convincing argument for those who are not acquainted with tithing to note the increase in his salary. However, the tithing was not undertaken with any thought of selfish gain."

When the church needed funds and suggestions of bazaars and fairs were given, Charles Cowman stood and opposed the suggestions, making a passionate appeal for the adoption of the scriptural plan. A Tithing League was formed and successfully carried out. The financial problem was promptly solved. There was no more need of worldly methods of fund raising. More important, the spiritual life of the church began to increase and a revival broke out at once.

Later Cowman decided to give all income to God, except what was needed for personal needs. Needs and wants were carefully weighed and the question asked, "How much can we do without this month?" They lived in a beautiful, well-furnished home, but exchanged it for a small apartment in order to support another native worker in Africa. When asked how he could afford to support so many native workers he replied, "I cannot afford it; I can sacrifice it."

At one of the great missionary conventions at the Moody Church the call of God gripped his heart. As the offering was taken to meet the great needs of foreign missions, Cowman placed on the plate a roll of bills representing his monthly salary together with his beautiful gold watch. After the offering the appeal was made for volunteers. Mr. and Mrs. Cowman offered themselves. They were later sent as missionaries to Japan.[5]

Dedication of Communists a Challenge

Some of the stories of the zeal of communists for their cause should challenge us as Christians.

According to one story a young communist was selling communist literature. It was cold and the young man was barefoot. Someone asked him, "Why don't you get yourself a pair of shoes?" He answered, "I cannot afford a pair of shoes when so many people do not know about communism." How often have we seen that kind of Christian dedication?

A friend of mine, now a minister of the gospel, told of his experience. He was born and educated in Russia.

225

When a senior in a communist college of 400 students, he and a friend were the only professing Christians. It was shortly after the communists had taken over. One day he and his chum were called into the principal's office. On his desk lay a revolver. He said, "You young men can give up your Christianity or else." As I recall the story his chum lost his life, but my friend went into hiding and by a miracle of God escaped the country.

He told us of the dedication of the Russian youth for communism. On May Day they march down the street singing:

"With the hammer and the sickle we must go forth to save the world. We must labor, toil, and fight; we must suffer, bleed and die, Till the victory is won."

He declared that some of those young communists would give 36 percent of their income to promote communism. They would throw themselves into a barbed wire entanglement and let their buddies climb over their torn bodies that communism might have victory.

As Christians we have a cause worth dying for, worth sacrificing for, yet many think that giving 10 percent is too great a sacrifice.

14

PROMOTING STEWARDSHIP

"We have been baptized into Christ's body by the one Spirit, and have all been given that same Holy Spirit" (1 Cor. 12:13, *The Living Bible*).

When Christ took on an earthly body, God was in Christ restoring the world to Himself. The world He had created, including man, became corrupt and estranged from God because of sin. The community of righteousness that God wanted could not be realized with sinful men. The incarnation and Calvary made possible man's redemption and his justification.

These redeemed people became the new people of God, the body of Christ. By the Spirit they have been baptized into one body, the church of Christ. This body composed of many members is commissioned to carry on His work. The ministry of reconciliation is given them. In Christ's stead they minister and help restore men to God's image.

"For God was in Christ, restoring the world to himself, no longer counting men's sins against them but blotting them out. This is the wonderful message he has given us to tell others. We are Christ's ambassadors. God is using us to speak to you: we beg you, as though Christ himself were here pleading with you, receive the love he offers you — be reconciled to God" (2 Cor. 5:19, 20, *The Living Bible*).

In Christ's stead the church of Christ ministers and proclaims the gospel. In His stead we bring men and women into His kingdom and lead them to Christian maturity. We are God's stewards in restoring the world to God and helping prepare a people, a community of love.

As the body of Christ, the church must be the lips of Jesus proclaiming His message. The church must be His hands ministering and serving. It must be His ears listening to the sighs, the groans, and the wants of people. The church must be the heart of Jesus, loving people, having compassion on them, sharing their sorrows and their joys.

Our Lord has the same love and compassion that He had when He lived on earth. He still loves people and wants to minister to their needs and to preach to them the gospel of the kingdom. The only way He can do this is through His body, and the members of His body. He wants to love, to redeem, and minister to people through us. This is the stewardship He has committed to us.

The Body of Christ Ministering

A number of years ago I saw the hands of Jesus feeding the hungry children in Hong Kong. I saw Him ministering to poverty-stricken refugees in Calcutta. He was doing this through a relief agency promoted by His churches. In the jungles of India I heard the lips of Jesus proclaiming the gospel of the kingdom to the Hindus. This He was doing through the members of His body, the missionaries. In mission hospitals I witnessed Christ healing lepers through Christian doctors and nurses. I saw Him open the eyes of the blind as Christian doctors removed cataracts from eyes of people who could not see. This is truly stewardship of the gospel, promoting the purposes of our Lord. Through this ministry of love by our Lord through His people, I also witnessed persons confess Christ and ask for baptism.

The interests of Jesus must be the interests of His body. As the Father sent the Son into the world, so the Son sends His followers. Jesus was sent to heal broken hearts, to preach deliverance, to set at liberty the bruised, to heal the blind, and to preach the gospel to the poor. This is the commission, the stewardship of the church. The church must be involved in ministering to the sorrows, the hurts, the bondage, the ignorance, and the poverty in our world.

Too often the church has been so engrossed in its ritual, its doctrines, and its programs that it has not had time to be the church — it failed in its primary stewardship. Many countries overrun by godless communism were countries where the church was present, in name at least. But was it really the church? Was it the body of Christ meeting the needs of people?

One Christian leader stated that just at the time when revolution was being fomented in Russia there was dire need, but the church was not awake to that need. In the face of grave danger the church was not aware of the dangers. At that time of need, and as revolution was about to break out, the religious leaders were wrestling with the problem of how often the bells should ring while the mass was being celebrated. Too often the main concern of the church has been quite irrelevant to the needs of the hour and to the primary purposes of God.

What are the stewardship implications for the church today in the problems of poverty? Of city slums and ghettos? Of militarism? Of race? Will stewardship of the gospel be concerned with the starving in Bangladesh? The refugees in Vietnam? The Middle East? The plight of minorities in America and Canada? Or, is this entirely irrelevant to Christian stewardship? Does stewardship begin and end with preaching the gospel?

Martin Luther is credited with saying that the only way to serve God is by helping meet the needs of people. I believe this is true. This is indicated by the Lord's parable of the judgment of the nations in Matthew 25. Those who failed in compassion and in ministering were cast out. While we must guard against our gospel becoming merely a social gospel, we must recognize that the gospel of Christ has some important social implications. Omitting the social implications our gospel is no longer the gospel of Christ.

Ministering to Human Needs Can Promote Evangelism

Ministering relief in the name of Christ can result in a strong evangelistic thrust. The primary purpose of ministering material aid to needy people should never be merely to add names to the church roll. Relief is offered in compassion to relieve hungry, suffering people. But when the love and compassion of Christ is shown through acts of kindness, persons will become more receptive to the gospel.

During the 1940s the church began a program of relief and service in an underprivileged part of Puerto Rico. Health and educational facilities were provided and an economical development program inaugurated. The Mennonite Conference of Puerto Rico has emerged with a dozen or more churches. From these churches have come pastors, teachers, and nurses. Living conditions have improved measurably.

About the same time the church became concerned

about the needs among the Spanish-speaking people in southern Texas. A group of Voluntary Service people were sent to minister to them. A small maternity hospital was built and nurses sent to help out. Clubs were formed for children and youth. Today there are a half dozen Spanish-speaking churches as a result.

There are growing churches in the Philippines, in Ethiopia, in Saigon, in Hong Kong, and in other places as a result of this type of stewardship. While the work was begun as a ministry to human needs, the intention from the start was to include a spiritual ministry, to minister to the whole person. This is what true stewardship of the gospel must do.

The Church Practicing Stewardship of the Gospel

One is thrilled when he reads the Book of Acts. Here is Christian stewardship at its very best. The church has never been able to surpass what we find in the Book of Acts. The apostles had witnessed the crucifixion and resurrection of the Lord and had received the baptism of the Spirit. Before Jesus had left them He commissioned them to go into all the world to make disciples and instruct them. They lost little time getting started, for to them had been committed a stewardship.

In the first seven chapters we see stewardship in the local church. There were great sermons and dynamic witnessing. "With great power gave the apostles witness of the resurrection of the Lord." They gave themselves to prevailing prayer. Signs and wonders were performed by the apostles. Those who had possessions sold them and brought the price and laid it at the apostles' feet, and there were none that lacked. Provision was made for the neglected widows. The membership of the church multiplied, 3000 at one time, a multitude of both men and women at another time, and the Lord was adding daily to the church. They gladly endured persecution for the sake of Christ.

The next five chapters have to do with the outreach of the gospel in surrounding areas. The great things that happened as the disciples ministered in and about Jerusalem forced them to take the gospel to neighboring areas. We find them in Damascus, Samaria, Joppa, Caesarea, Antioch, and elsewhere. Revivals followed and numbers were added to their fellowship, including despised Samaritans and Gentiles. This caused the believers to take another look at evangelism, at stewardship of the gospel. Must persons of other cultures conform to Jewish patterns?

As the church at Antioch ministered and prayed, the Spirit said, "Separate me Barnabas and Saul for the work whereunto I have called them" (Acts 13:2). The remainder of the Book of Acts has to do with stewardship of the gospel in foreign missions. It is a story of God's stewards dedicating themselves to the purposes of God, suffering hardship and privations, witnessing with the Spirit's power. Churches were established and multitudes of people were won to the Christian faith and instructed in the doctrines of Christ.

This example of commitment and of the zeal of the early church should spur us on to more effective stewardship of the gospel — winning men to faith in Christ, instructing them in His ways, and ministering to their needs.

Being an Informed Church

"Look around you! Vast fields of human souls are ripening all around us, and are ready now for reaping. The reapers will be paid good wages and will be gathering eternal souls into the granaries of heaven! What joys await the sower and the reaper, both together!" (Jn. 4:35-37, *The Living Bible*).

The church must constantly be looking out on the fields and informing its members of the great needs of the world and the open doors for evangelism and service. An uniformed church will not be an evangelistic church. It will not be a giving church. Unless people know what the needs are and what the church is doing to meet those needs, it cannot pray intelligently for those needs. The church will not likely give itself to meet those needs. They will not give generously of their means for the cause.

Through missionary speakers, church periodicals, church bulletins, the pastor and mission representative and in other ways members must be kept informed. An informed and committed congregation will generously support the work of the church. The members must be kept aware that they are doing something grander and far greater than giving to a budget or meeting quotas; they are engaged in mission; they are ministering to human needs; they are promoting the kingdom of God.

Stewardship of Accumulated Wealth

Not only must the church challenge its members to support the cause of Christ with their tithes and offerings, but to be good stewards of accumulated wealth. There is a tremendous service here that the church can provide for its members, but in which it has badly failed in the past. As a result hundreds of thousands of dollars that could have served the purposes of God and could have been treasures laid up in heaven, have been lost as far as the church is concerned. Millions that should have gone for kingdom purposes have been lost in taxes, court costs, attorney's fees, and sometimes to ungrateful heirs.

The church owes it to its members to instruct them about responsible stewardship. Pastors should be concerned that members of their churches are aware of ways open to them to secure their funds for worthy causes, as well as for the good of their families. They should help their members be "rich toward God." Pastors should be aware of information and services available to their members from their mission boards and denominational headquarters.

Mennonite Foundation

The Mennonite brotherhood some years ago established Mennonite Foundation, Inc. This is a service agency emphasizing effective stewardship of accumulated possessions. It has offices in Winnipeg and Kitchener in Canada, and in Lancaster, Pennsylvania, Goshen, Indiana, and Hesston, Kansas. The personnel serving the Foundation consider themselves servants to persons and congregations. Special stewardship conferences and seminars are held in many places. The theme of the meetings is "Partnership in Discipleship" or "Effective Stewardship of Accumulated Possessions." They talk about and give information on wills, investments, life income gift plans, taxes, estate planning, etc.

The Foundation works closely with church institutions, colleges, mission boards, relief agencies and others, especially in the area of special and deferred gift programs. The Foundation is not in competition with the institutions but is a helper, facilitator, an advisory resource.

The Foundation gives high priority to urging every adult member of the church to have a will and keep it up to date. To leave the disposition of possessions and the care of loved ones to a secular court is unfaithful stewardship.

A unique service rendered is that of distributing charitable bequests. Many make their bequests to Mennonite Foundation. On a separate form they state how they want the bequest distributed. They are at liberty to change these from time to time. Adjustments can be made without changing the will. This provides flexibility for the donors.

There is a wide variety of life income plans. In these the donor receives a lifetime income. After his death the charitable remainder is distributed to the institutions or causes that he had specified. The causes he wants to support may be changed at any time during his life.

A person may want to make a charitable contribution, for tax or any other purpose, but is not yet certain where he wants it to go. He may transfer property or cash to a Gift Deposit Plan. He receives the charitable contribution deduction the year the transfer is made. Later on, at his convenience, he can by voucher or "check" draw on that deposit for a contribution to any church institution or charitable organization recognized by IRS.

The Mennonite Foundation is approved by IRS but should not be confused with private foundations. The restrictions placed on private foundations by the Tax Reform Act of 1969 do not apply to Mennonite Foundation. It enjoys the most generous tax advantages and incentives which exist under the IRS code.

The Foundation sees the investment of church money as a serious responsibility and attempts to exercise leadership in this area. It is constantly developing and refining moral and social guidelines.

The Foundation does not pressure people to make gifts to church-related causes. Their aim is to help people exercise good stewardship of possessions. They will assist individuals in estate planning even though the church may not be a beneficiary.

Foundation gifts and assets have increased more than ten times in the past five years. Hundreds of thousands of dollars have been directed to church institutions and to the Lord's work. Hundreds of people have been helped to joyful stewardship experiences. Millions in treasures have been laid up in heaven through this service agency. An increasing number of persons and churches are asking for the services of the Foundation and are finding effective ways of being good stewards of possessions.

Persons of other denominations no doubt can find comparable services by getting in touch with their denominational headquarters. Effective stewardship of accumulated possessions should be a concern of every responsible member of Christ's church, and should be a concern of the church.

Supporting Religious Rackets

The most despicable of rackets is the religious racket. There are scores of them in our world. Unscrupulous men play on the sympathies and compassion of charitable people, misrepresenting and fabricating to wring money out of them for selfish purposes. Millions of dollars are given every year by good-meaning people to phony causes. Hundreds of church members are regular contributors, believing they are helping worthy causes, yet are pouring their money down the drain. How tragic when their own mission boards and church institutions are hurting for lack of funds!

Last week I received a letter from a church leader who said, "Every week I learn of some agency that is engaged in unethical practices and which is succeeding in attracting support from our people." Swindling church members who want to support the gospel and help the needy becomes a lucrative business for many selfish and unscrupulous people. Our mails constantly bring to us appeals for money. There are pictures of starving children, orphans, or evangelists who need support. These play on our emotions and naturally we would like to help.

Some of these agencies have been investigated. Many

of them will not give an audited report. Some will not answer inquiries as to where their missions or institutions are. Others use the major part of funds received for overhead, less than 50 percent going for the purpose for which it was given. When your own church has missions, charitable institutions, and relief services why send your money to questionable causes? Too many people feel, mistakenly, that their money does more good in outside causes.

A few years ago a generous man wanted to send relief to a foreign country. He was told by an agency that for $800 they would deliver a carload of food. He thought that was good and decided to do it. But he first asked relief agents of his own denomination. These men said, "Give us the $800 and we will send two carloads, and in every package there will be some literature from our denominational headquarters." He sent the relief through his own church.

There was an agency in Kansas City that widely publicized its work in the Holy Lands. This, of course, had great appeal for many people. I was in a home that had recently sent them $50. I was in another home where they had a check ready to send. I said, "I wouldn't give a cent to that outfit," and told them why. Because of his scandalous conduct the founder was not permitted to re-enter or work in the Holy Land, according to a statement from Christian leaders in and about Jerusalem. According to this report, contrary to his claims, he had no blind home in Jordan, he had no leper work there, he had no mobile clinic, no trade school, and no missionaries to teach Bible. Yet, he was soliciting and receiving large amounts of money to support these nonexistent causes. Sympathy-provoking propaganda was distributed widely that moved hundreds to give. It was reported that he had as many as eight or nine sponsors for single orphans. When the *Gospel Herald* warned its readers against supporting this cause and exposed some false claims the *Herald* was threatened with a libel suit if it did not publish a retraction. No retraction was published and there was no libel suit.

Another Example

A missionary from South America, where there was an effective program of indigenous mission work carried on by the church among an Indian tribe, told how a "fly by night" missionary came through and advertised a meeting. Those attending were promised all the barbequed beef they could eat. At the appointed time a large group of people assembled. Naturally there was much merriment, as everyone enjoyed the barbequed beef. After the meal the "missionary" spoke forcefully about Jesus Christ. He asked those who wanted to follow Jesus to raise their hands. Many of them did not know what it meant to follow Jesus, but if it meant barbequed beef they were for it. There was a good response.

"All right," said the missionary, "those of you who raised your hands come to the river for baptism." He had pictures taken of himself baptizing a "convert" with a long line waiting to be baptized. The picture was good propaganda for raising funds for this "faith missionary." No doubt members of the church that had an effective program of evangelism, upon seeing that picture, would say, "That's where we want our money to go. That is missions." The Indians he baptized may never have seen him again. He was not building churches or building people up in Christ. The responsible steward will be careful that his offerings go to worthy causes.

Do not let pictures of poor starving and crippled people move you to give to the cause that is distributing them. There may be a good chance that they never saw the person pictured but got the picture and are trying to get mileage out of it. A few years ago a group doing work among lepers were showing pictures in an effort to raise funds. A missionary from another church was present and saw a picture he recognized at once as being taken at the leper clinic of his church. The other group had somehow got hold of the picture and was using it for publicity purposes.

Moneys Worth, a consumer newsletter from New York in its August 21, 1971, letter had an article entitled "Charities for Suckers." It states that in many cases worthy-sounding philanthropic causes are operated mainly for the benefit of the operating agency. This has become a 21 billion dollar a year business. In some cases the overhead is 90 cents of every dollar contributed. Some charitable organizations to which many people like to give have tens of millions of dollars in cash and securities, according to *Moneys Worth.* Father Flanagan's Boys Town, called by an Omaha newspaper, "a money machine," has more than $200 million laid away, yet continues to receive from investments and contributions 25 million annually. This is 400% more than is needed to care for 700 boys, according to the above source.

There are so many needy and worthy causes to which to give and yet so many millions of dollars are given where it is not really needed and to causes the donors would not want to support if they knew all the facts. A good steward will not only give generously but he will want to make sure that his contributions go for the most worthy causes. How can one determine what causes to support?

1. Be sure that you are supporting the work of your own church before supporting outside causes.

2. Do not be taken in too easily with dramatic fund-raising appeals. Make sure before you subscribe that your

money will go where you want it.

3. Before you give largely to any cause insist on seeing an audited financial report. Any reputable organization should not hesitate to give a report. Supporters of a cause have a right to know how the money is used. Some questionable agencies refuse to give audited reports.

4. Find out what percent of your dollar goes for the purpose you give. One widely publicized world mission absorbs the larger part of the dollar in overhead. It no doubt is doing some good work, but do you want 60 cents of your dollar paying high-salaried officers and high-pressure publicity?

Recently the following note appeared in a mission newsletter.

> *"Take note on the efficiency ratings of aid programs:* When you give $100 to help other people, it costs $300 to deliver that $100 worth of aid through federal channels . . . $27 to deliver the same amount through voluntary charities . . . and $8 to deliver it through the church . . . (from statistics compiled for the Better Business Bureau by the National Association of Life Underwriters in Washington, D.C.).

5. Don't send money in response to a telephone call unless you know the ones to whom it is sent.

6. The National Information Bureau suggests that we should never give to organizations that send unordered gifts (I receive on the average more than one a week). The fund-raising costs of these usually is exorbitant — sometimes as much as 90 cents out of each dollar. These "gifts" are sent to make you feel guilty if you do not respond with cash. Often fund-raising organizations furnish the list of names and addresses for their clients and do the mailing. The cause represented gets only a small percent of what you send.

7. If in doubt better not give until you have investigated. The executive secretary of your mission board can perhaps advise as to the worthiness of the cause or find out for you whether it is a reputable agency.

8. Remember that when you support with your tithes and offerings your local church budget you are giving to world missions, relief, Christian education, and broadcasting as well as to the support of your local program. You are not merely giving to a budget; you are supporting missions, giving to needs of people, and giving to the Lord.

Responsible stewardship on the part of the church demands that through its mission board, its official organ, and its pastors it keeps its members informed of opportunities to serve and support the work of their own church. They should be made aware of worthy causes and challenged to support them. They should be taught that responsible stewardship of possessions begins when one starts earning and does not end until the estate is settled or arrangements have been made for the use of accumulated possessions.

It is also the duty of the church to caution its members against giving to unworthy causes, to religious rackets. The possessions that God entrusts to Christians should be used for Christian causes and not carelessly given to unworthy causes.

15

THE RESPONSIBLE STEWARD

The needs of the world and the needs of God's kingdom are great. The bounteous gifts and resources that God has entrusted to man are just as great, and in the hands of responsible people would meet the great needs of the kingdom and of the world. The blessings of God for responsible stewardship are tremendous and the penalties for unfaithfulness severe. There is every reason why as Christians we should take seriously the stewardship committed to us by God. We should be concerned in being responsible stewards and in promoting responsible stewardship in the community of God.

Characteristics of the Responsible Steward

1. Like the Macedonians, the steward will first give himself to the Lord. He will believe in his heart and confess with his lips that Jesus is Savior and Lord.

2. He will recognize the lordship of Christ, that he has been crucified with Christ and that Christ lives in him. "I have been put to death with Christ on the cross, so that it is no longer I who live, but it is Christ who lives in me" (Gal. 2:20, TEV). Only as Christ lives within and controls

our lives can we really be responsible stewards of God.

We are inclined to pray, "Lord, help me in my work. Help me live the Christian life." I don't believe He wants to help us do these things. He wants to do them in and through us. In my early ministry, before preaching a sermon I would pray, "Lord, help me give the message these people need." I don't do that anymore. Rather I pray, "Lord, have complete control of my mind, of my heart, and of my lips. Give Your message to these people through me." I believe He wants to speak through us, minister through us, live the holy life in us, generously support the stewardship of the gospel, and meet the needs of the world through us. The responsible steward is controlled by the Spirit of the living Christ. The will of the Lord becomes his will also.

3. By the Spirit of God the steward is baptized into Christ's body, the church. The responsible steward is a loyal member of the church. Just as Jesus loved the church and gave Himself for it, so His people will love the church and give themselves for it. They will use their talents and gifts for the good of the body and for the promotion of the work of their Lord. Their loyalty, or lack of loyalty, to the church will portray their loyalty or lack of loyalty to their Lord.

When Saul of Tarsus was persecuting the church and making havoc of it he was smitten down by the Lord who asked, "Saul, Saul, why are you persecuting me?" Saul thought he was persecuting the church, but the Lord said, "Saul, you are persecuting me." As he persecuted the body of Christ he was persecuting Christ Himself.

As we fail in our love and support of the church, Christ's body, we fail in love and support of Christ. On the other hand, as we love the church and are loyal to it we are loyal to our Lord. This must be true when the church is truly the church, the body of Christ engaged in His work. Even with all its imperfections Christ is carrying on His work in the world through His church. The church is far from irrelevant in today's world. It is the most relevant body in existence, made up of the true stewards of God. Christ dwells in His body and will present it to Himself without blemish.

The church today is often discounted, criticized, and maligned. Due to inconsistencies and carnality in members of the body of Christ, the body is discredited. But the church remains Christ's body and is destined to reign with Him. The responsible steward will be loyal to the Head of the church and concerned with the welfare of every member of the body. Instead of criticizing the body he will strive to help the members to be faithful. The failure is not in the Head of the church, nor is it in the divine body of Christ, but in the human members that compose that body.

4. The responsible steward will promote the fellowship of the saints and be subject to the counsel of his brethren and the church. His attitude will be like the apostles when they said, "It seemed good to the Holy Spirit and to us." The individualist who says, "It seemed good to me and the Holy Spirit," is too often a dangerous leader trying to drive instead of lead.

It is significant that in each of the Lord's messages to the seven churches in the Book of Revelation He concludes with, "He that hath an ear, let him hear what the Spirit saith unto the churches." Not "What the Spirit says to him." God spoke to Saul on the Damascus road, but he was told what to do by a representative of the church through the voice of the Spirit. It was the leaders of the church that asked him to help in the work at Antioch. The Spirit through the church at Antioch commissioned Paul and Barnabas for their missionary journey.

The person who is subject to the church and is commissioned by the church is much more likely to be a servant of the church and of God's people. The one who feels called of God and needs no commission from the church will more likely be a boss, a bigot, or a dictator rather than a servant. The responsible steward will be subject to the church of Christ.

5. The responsible steward will be generous in sharing and using his possessions to promote the work of the church and to meet the needs of his brothers and sisters. He will give in proportion as God gives to him. Someone has said that each pay check is a new Eden. Do we recognize God's ownership and His claim to a portion for His purposes? Or do we feel that "all the trees of the garden" are ours? "If then, you have not been faithful in handling worldly wealth, how can you be trusted with true wealth?" (Lk. 16:11, TEV).

6. The true steward will be engaged in bringing others into a new life with Christ and into the fellowship of the church. If right relationship with Christ and membership in His church are truly meaningful to us, we will want others to know these joys and blessings. It would be an indictment against our spiritual experience if we were not concerned in bringing others to Christ and into the fellowship of the saints. Evidently the Christian life is not very meaningful to us if we are not eager to have others enjoy it.

God's stewards will use the resources God has given them in reconciling lost men to God, helping them to become a new creation in Christ. They will realize, however, that this is but the beginning. The Great Commission obligates us not only to make disciples, but also to instruct them in the "all things" of Christ. Babes in Christ must be nurtured to manhood. There is joy in heaven when a sinner turns to Christ, but there must be grief when he remains a babe instead of growing to Christian manhood.

Jesus was grateful for the disciples the Father had given Him, yet He agonized in prayer in their behalf that they might be kept from evil, that they might be one, and that they might be perfect. As a responsible steward of God, Paul was deeply concerned with the spiritual growth of the believers. He prayed day and night with tears. He wrote letters of rebuke, instruction, and encouragement. Perfecting the saints was a vital part of stewardship of the gospel as far as Paul was concerned. It must be a deep concern of responsible stewards today.

7. The steward, like his Lord, will have compassion upon the multitudes. Because of the love of his Lord he cannot be insensitive to the pangs of hungry stomachs, the hurting wounds of injustice and discrimination, the despair of war refugees, the cries of the victims of disasters, and the agonies of the downtrodden. He will be giving the cup of cold water in the name of Christ. He will be pouring oil on the wounds of society. He will be giving the bread of compassion to his hungry brothers. Like the Apostle Paul, he will be stirring up the brotherhood in behalf of the needs of those who are of the "household of faith."

Indifference on the part of God's people to the suffering and cries of the oppressed and the needy in Old Testament times evoked severe rebukes from the prophets of God. Irresponsibility to needs of people and lack of compassion called for severe punishment in the parables of our Lord. One cannot be a responsible steward of God without a real concern and compassion for God's people in need.

8. The trustworthy steward will have his financial house in order, having made provision that any accumulated wealth entrusted to him will also serve the purposes of God. It is nothing short of tragic when a follower of Christ,

who has been entrusted with earthly possessions, makes no provision for its use after he is gone. Millions of dollars entrusted to Christians by God to promote His kingdom are lost and do not serve useful purposes because of careless stewardship. What could have meant untold blessings and treasures laid up in heaven is instead destroyed by rust and eaten by worms, because men were not trustworthy stewards.

Every person entrusted with wealth should realize that it is a trust to be administered for good. Even if one gave generously as he was earning he is still responsible for the proper management of accumulated possessions. Through a will or in some other way provision should be made for the proper use of possessions should the possessor be called from this life. The question, "Then whose shall those things be, which thou hast provided?" should be satisfactorily answered before the end of life comes.

It is generally recognized that every adult person should have a will. He should have a will for the sake of his family. Many widows have experienced great hardships because the deceased husband had left no will. Recently I read of a young widow left with a small son. The husband had not realized the importance of a will or had carelessly neglected making one. Until the court could meet and act this widow had no money for funeral expenses, no money for living expenses, and the son was a ward of the court all because the husband had neglected something very important.

As a responsible steward he will want to have a will to make sure that what has been entrusted to him will continue to serve God's purposes after he is gone. Many Christians intend to do this but never get it done. One minister tried to show a millionaire the importance of a will. He promised he would take care of it. Some time later the minister heard of the death of this man and asked whether he had a will. The answer was that he had never got around to it. The courts had to make disposition of what God had entrusted to him.

Recently I have heard of several active Christian men who have considerable assets, but no will. They are past middle age and are considering having wills drawn up. But will they get it done before it is too late?

The Christian's will should not overlook the Lord who is the giver of wealth. One man took his will to a Christian attorney who examined it and said, "You have left out your best friend." The man asked whom he had left out. The attorney replied, "You have left out the Lord Jesus. He is the one who has given all you have." The man saw his mistake and changed the will to include the church of Christ.

Recently a woman said to a friend, "For years my husband and I have had wills but we never thought of remembering Christ in our wills. We are going to change them." Some Christians specify 10 percent for the church, the mission board, or a church institution. Others remember the church with an amount equal to the heirs mentioned in the will.

The Example of a School Administrator

"My wife and I have reciprocal but identical wills, a recommendation in this state. Our children are all college graduates and either have positions or are getting the education for positions which should allow them to have a reasonable degree of financial independence. They will not depend on an inheritance for their personal financial planning. We have included three church institutions in our wills on the same basis as our children." See Appendix on the making of a will.

Giving Guides for Christian Stewards

John H. Rudy, President of Mennonite Foundation, Inc., Goshen, Indiana, gives the following giving guides for Christian stewards.

There are many ways to contribute in the work of the Lord. Our tax laws provide you with a variety of methods to stretch your gift dollars and to make them do more good. As a Christian steward you will want to know how you can give most efficiently. Less for taxes, more for the church.

Tax deductions reduce the cost of your gift to the church. Your actual out-of-pocket cost may be much less than you realize. The higher your income, the lower your cost. In addition, there may eventually be substantial savings in estate tax, inheritance tax, and administration expense, since lifetime gifts remove assets from your taxable estate.

Give out of a heart of love and gratitude to God in response to His extravagance toward you. Give to extend the cause of Christ. But try to give economically. Give as much mileage as you can from what you give. Consider the tax implications. The way you give may determine how much you can give. As a concerned steward you may find some helpful guidance among the giving methods described below:

1. *Give property as well as cash.* Don't stop giving cash. Give all you can. But there are excellent ways to expand your giving program by transferring property to church agencies. You can give almost any kind of property: stocks, bonds, mutual fund shares, houses, farmland. The amount of your gift is based on the fair market value of the property on the date of transfer. Property gifts may offer you a whole new array of giving opportunities.

249

2. *Give property which has increased in value.* There is a much better way than selling your property, paying the capital gains tax, and giving what's left. For example, property you own may be worth $10,000, based on the present fair market value. Let's assume your cost is $6,000. Here is what you can do: You can give the property to a church agency. This entitles you to an income tax deduction for the present value of $10,000. What's more, you pay no tax on the gain of $4,000. And the church agency is exempt from this tax, too.

3. *Give with an awareness of tax implications.* Tax laws actually encourage giving to charitable organizations. For example, you can take an income tax deduction for all gifts to church agencies. Cash gifts can be deducted up to 50 percent of adjusted gross income. The limit for property gifts is 30 percent. And any excess beyond these limits can be carried forward for five successive years. Lifetime gifts, either to the children or to the church, may eventually mean substantial savings in estate and inheritance taxes.

4. *Give the profit by selling at your cost.* This is often referred to as a bargain sale gift plan. Let's say you have property which cost you $6,000. Its market value is now $10,000. You may be able to arrange a "bargain sale" to a church agency at your cost of $6,000. You get back your original investment. You have given the profit of $4,000 for which you are entitled to an income tax deduction. You will, however, need to pay capital gains tax on part of the gain.

5. *Give property but reserve its present use.* This is like keeping your property while you give it away. It works like this: You transfer title to your personal residence or farm to a church agency. By way of a life estate contract you reserve the right to use the property and to receive any income as long as you live. You are entitled to an in-

come tax deduction in the year you transfer the property, based on the "present value" of the gift. There may eventually be additional savings in estate and inheritance taxes.

6. *Give and receive fixed income for life.* You may wish you could give more to the work of the Lord. But you can't. You need income on your money to live. There are some very attractive methods for giving cash or property and then receiving a guaranteed fixed income for life. These methods are often referred to as gift annuity agreements and charitable remainder annuity trusts. Payment rates range between 4 percent and 10 percent, with the specific rate depending upon your age and the nature of your gift property. There are often significant tax savings.

7. *Give and receive variable income for life.* You can transfer cash or property into gift plans known as life income agreements and charitable remainder unitrusts. The lifetime income to you will vary from year to year depending upon actual investment yield or the market value of the assets. There may be significant tax savings.

8. *Give and retain the right to withdraw.* You can deposit cash in a revocable deposit gift agreement. Or property can be transferred to a revocable charitable remainder trust. Income from these plans is paid to you for life. You retain the right to take back the cash or property anytime you choose. There are no income tax savings. But any amount remaining in the plans at your death entitles your estate to a charitable deduction.

9. *Give now and distribute later.* Cash or property can be transferred to a separate gift deposit account administered for you by the Mennonite Foundation. This entitles you to an income tax deduction in the year you make the transfer to the Foundation. Sometime later, at your convenience, you can tell the Foundation how you want

251

these gift funds distributed. It works much like a checking account. You can specify distribution to any church institution or other charitable organization recognized by Internal Revenue Service.

10. *Give from your estate by your will.* You may be among those who are quite limited in their ability to give to the work of the Lord during their lifetimes. But you may want to consider the giving opportunities which you have through your will. Many people are tithing their estates. Others are adopting the church as one of their children. Still other people, with no children or with no pressing needs among their children, are designating larger parts of their estates for the work of the church. Everything included in a will for church causes is exempt from federal estate tax. You do need a will of your own!

11. *Give to members of your family.* Aside from your giving to the church, there may be legitimate needs among your children. The best time to offer financial help may be right now, when the needs are the greatest, long before you pass away and your will takes effect. Our tax laws allow you to give up to $3,000 per year to each of your children, and you owe no gift tax. This "annual exclusion" becomes $6,000 per year per person when both husband and wife consent to the gift. Tax-free giving within the family is possible even beyond these annual limits by employing your once-and-done "lifetime exemption" of $30,000; this becomes $60,000 when husband and wife make the gift together. In some cases it may be advisable to incur gift tax in order to save much larger amounts in estate tax and administration costs.

Let your giving be a generous response to God's lavish love toward you. And let it be an expression of your commitment to Jesus Christ. But let the tax laws reduce the "cost" of your giving. Use tax savings to increase the size

252

of your gifts. The giving methods described above may help you save more so that you can give more. Give efficiently!

❀ ❀ ❀

The Steward Will Provide for His Own

The suggestions given in this chapter are by no means intended to leave the impression that heirs should be excluded for the sake of religious purposes. A Christian should think first of all of the needs of his family as consideration is being given to disposition of possessions. To neglect members of his family in order to give to the needs of others` would not be responsible stewardship.

On the other hand, a large inheritance may be a curse to an heir instead of a blessing. Before willing large amounts of money to any heir it is well to ask two questions: "Will my heir be safe with that amount of money," and, "Will my money be safe in the hands of this heir?" If both questions cannot be answered in the affirmative one should have second thoughts about it.

The responsible steward will also ask, "Where will my possessions do the most good?" Money bequeathed to heirs who have already more than they can profitably use is wasted money. Recently an elderly lady with considerable wealth wanted to draw up a will (something she had far too long neglected). Her only direct heir was a daughter who had nearly reached the years of retirement and whose assets nearly equaled that of her mother. When asked whom she wanted as beneficiary of her estate the elderly lady replied, "My daughter has been good to me. I want to leave my possessions to her." Was that responsible stewardship?

Why should she burden her daughter with more wealth when already she had more than she would ever need? Wouldn't responsible stewardship demand that a good share at least be dedicated to the needs of people and to promote the kingdom of Christ?

Words of Wisdom from Wise Fathers

"The almighty dollar bequeathed to children is an almighty curse. No man has the right to handicap his son with such a burden as great wealth." — *Andrew Carnegie.*

"I wouldn't have my children deprived of the fun and benefit of wanting something and going out to fight for it." — *Dr. William Mayo.*

"We are striving and even slaving to lay up property for our children when statistics clearly show that the more we lay up for them, the worse off they are going to be. If statistics demonstrate any one thing, they demonstrate that the less money we leave our children, the better they will be off." — *Roger W. Babson.*

"I've lost the chance of giving a million or two to my children, or to somebody else, but it may be that I have helped them far more than I have hindered them. I have known not a few men who have cursed their descendants for generations by large inheritances." — *A. A. Hyde.*

"It is well-nigh impossible for a very rich man to defend his children from the habits of self-indulgence, laziness, and selfishness." — *Dr. Elliot, President-Emeritus of Harvard.*

Fountains of Blessing or Whirlpools of Destruction

God told Israel, "Behold, I set before you this day a blessing and a curse." That is what God does each time He entrusts man with material wealth. That wealth can be a tremendous blessing to him, to society, and to the glory of God. It can also be a curse, drowning men in perdition and destruction.

With the talents and rich resources God has given us

we can become fountains of blessing or whirlpools of destruction. Fountains are symbols of self-giving, imparting life to flowers, grass, and trees, filling the air with freshness. They make glad the hearts of man, animals, and birds, adding life and beauty to nature.

On the other hand, whirlpools are a symbol of base selfishness, capturing everything that comes within their gyrations, greedily engulfing them and drawing them into the black deep from whence they do not return.

While such are few in our seas and rivers, unfortunately there are many of them in the sea of society. True self-love and selfhood are degraded into selfishness which becomes the center of their lives. They live not for God's glory nor for the welfare of men, but only for self. Ego is the center of their universe. They sacrifice the glory of God and the welfare of their fellowmen at the shrine of self-interest.

As far as they are concerned, poverty areas may remain poverty areas. Ghetto dwellers may continue in the ghettos, the hungry may remain hungry, so long as they themselves can continue to grow rich and have their selfish desires satisfied. They are content to build their own fortunes while the poverty-stricken remain in poverty. It may be individuals, or it may be organized commercial, political, or even religious groups that constitute these whirlpools, sucking their victims to dark despair. Commercial machines, political machines, ecclesiastical machines without compassion.

The one question these people ask is, "What will we get?" Judas belonged to this class. "What will you give me?" to betray the Son of God. The guards at Jesus' tomb also belonged, "And they took the money." Took the money to rob the world of the resurrection story! Men of whirlpool character ask, "What will you give me?" and

"They take the money." They take it to promote prostitution, drugs, alcoholism, war, gangsterism, anything that means money in their pockets, regardless of the suffering, poverty, death, and damnation it may mean to others.

It is these whirlpools that the prophets cry out against. Micah says, "Woe to you who lie awake at night, plotting wickedness; you rise up at dawn to carry out your schemes; because you can, you do. You want a certain piece of land, or someone else's house (though it is all he has); you take it by fraud and threats of violence" (2:1, 2, *The Living Bible*).

Amos cried out against Israel, "For they perverted justice by accepting bribes, and sold into slavery the poor who can't pay their debts; they trade them for a pair of shoes. They trample the poor in the dust and kick aside the meek" (2:6, 7, *The Living Bible*).

Or, listen to Zephaniah, "Her leaders are like roaring lions hunting their victims, out for everything they can get. Her judges are like ravening wolves at evening time, who by dawn have left no trace of their prey. Her prophets are liars seeking their own gain" (3:3, 4, *The Living Bible*).

Jesus saw the Pharisees as self-centered whirlpools, and pronounced a curse upon them for "devouring widows' houses."

But, thank God, there are also in our world fountains of blessing and springs of fresh waters. Instead of selfishly grasping for all they can get, they are freely giving out. In our society there are such refreshing fountains, although far too few. They are the men and women who have drunk from the Fountain of Living Waters, and have within themselves living streams. They have received freely and in turn are giving freely. They live for others and for God. Their big question is not, "What will I get?" but rather, "How much can I give? How can I help others?"

Jesus was the True Fountain. He came to give, and to give abundantly. The Apostle Paul was another fountain — giving, giving, giving — never asking what he was to receive. He was ready to spend and be spent that others might live. Barnabas was a fountain, selling his property and giving it to the church at Jerusalem that others might not lack.

After meeting Jesus, Zacchaeus was a fountain, giving half his goods to feed the poor. The Christians at Macedonia were fountains, first giving themselves, then out of deep poverty giving "beyond their power" to their needy brethren at Jerusalem.

Thank God for fountains of blessing in our churches today making possible an effective missions program, helping thousands to become new creatures in Christ. These fountains also make possible a ministry of compassionate relief and service, ministering to thousands of refugees and poverty-stricken people. These fountains are contributing significantly to the stewardship of the gospel.

Selfish covetous people are whirlpools of destruction. Generous giving persons are fountains of blessing.

Vertical and Horizontal Relationships

To be a responsible steward one must have right vertical and horizontal relationships. These relationships supplement each other and are dependent on each other. Unless one loves God and recognizes Him as Creator, Redeemer, Sustainer and as Lord, he will not love his fellowmen with *agape* love. He will not show proper regard for God's creation. Man's attitude toward God is reflected in his attitude toward man, God's creatures, and his environment.

The fall of man resulted not only in broken relationships between man and his God, but also between man and man, between man and other creatures, between man and his environment. Only complete restoration to the image of God will fully restore these broken relationships.

But man's attitude toward God's creation also reflects his attitude toward God, when he is at enmity with his fellowmen; when he ruthlessly slaughters God's creatures; when he exploits the soil, the forests, and other natural resources; when he pollutes the air, the water, and the earth; when he fails in recognizing God as Creator, Redeemer, and Lord. As we abuse God's children, His creatures, and His world, we dishonor God Himself.

The responsible steward will avoid two errors: first, that only the vertical relationship is important, and second, that only the horizontal relationship matters. Some would say that only the vertical relationship is really important. Have faith in Christ and a right attitude toward the Scriptures and be a member of a fundamental church. Little else matters. One can continue to be a racist, a materialist, a militarist, and be unconcerned in the plight of the world. The Sermon on the Mount and the parables and teachings of Jesus should show the folly of this type of pharisaism.

Others take the opposite attitude — the horizontal relationship is all that matters. Become engaged in social action. Have concern and compassion for the underprivileged and the needy of the world. Promote peace and brotherhood. What one believes about God and the Scriptures is not important.

The responsible steward will realize that both positions are unscriptural, unchristian and heretical. He will "take heed to himself and to the doctrine" (1 Tim. 4:16). His attitude toward man will reflect his attitude toward the Redeemer of men, and his attitude toward God's creation will reflect his attitude toward the Creator. Conversely, his attitude toward the Creator and Redeemer will be reflected in his relationships with man and the world.

As a responsible steward of God the Christian will be a faithful partner of his Lord in reconciling the world to God. Gladly will he dedicate talents and possessions in restoring broken relationships and promoting God's community of love in the earth.

Appendix

The following suggestions by John H. Rudy should be helpful to persons considering a will.

A WILL OF YOUR OWN

There are two ways to handle your postmortem stewardship responsibilities. You can let the state decide how your possessions should be distributed and what should happen to your loved ones. Or you can decide. You can have a will of your own. Every Christian steward, regardless of age or wealth, husband and wife, should have a Christian will. Only by making a Christian will can you be sure your desires are carried out after you're gone.

There are seven simple steps in making a Christian will. It's not at all complicated.

1. *List Your Possessions.* Take a careful look at what God has allowed you to accumulate. Check your property titles. Be concerned with present and future values, rather than original cost. Your estate will be appraised on the basis of market values at the time you pass away.

2. *Seek Divine Guidance.* How can you make your possessions go as far as possible and do the most good for your family and your church? Pray for wisdom. And you may need some technical assistance. When you make your will, you are making some of the most important decisions of your lifetime.

3. *Provide for Your Family.* With young children and a modest estate, you will want your survivors to receive as much as possible. In the event both parents are taken, a capable trustee will be needed to manage property for minor children. More important, guardians should be named, to make sure the children are raised in a Christian home.

4. *Remember the Church.* Perhaps you have no children. Or your children are grown and on their own. You are confronted with new opportunities among our mission boards, relief programs, hospitals, schools, and local congregations. You can use your Christian will, in many wonderful ways, to help further the cause of Christ.

5. *Consider Tax Savings.* Build into your will as many tax-saving features as you can. For example, everything you specify for the church is exempt from Federal Estate Tax. You can transfer up to one half of your estate to your surviving spouse tax-free. You may want to explore the use of trusts. Get as much mileage out of your estate as possible.

6. *Choose an Executor.* You will need someone to manage your affairs after you've gone, some competent person to settle your estate. You can name some qualified relative or friend. Or you can turn the job over to the trust department of a bank, a continuous, corporate executor capable of efficient management of possessions.

7. *Find a Good Lawyer.* Tell your attorney what you own and how you want your possessions distributed. Let him express your desires in the necessary legal language. You'll find his charge quite reasonable. Don't try to write your own will. If you have no lawyer, make some inquiries at the bank and among your business friends. You may also need the help of a tax accountant.

Without a will, the state in which you live will handle your affairs according to a general formula. Your own Christian convictions, your desires, the specific needs of your family, the needs of the church; none of these can be given the special consideration you would want. Neglect is never a virtue. This is especially true when it comes to your postmortem stewardship. Have a will of your own. Make it soon!

NOTES

Chapter 2

1. *Effective Workers in Needy Fields,* Student Voluntary Movement, 1902, p. 28.
2. Dr. Homer Homrighausen in address to meeting of Joint Department of Stewardship and Benevolence of NCC, Buckhill Falls, Pa., 1955.
3. Robert Hastings, Broadman Press, 1961, p. 4.
4. A. C. Conrad, *Divine Economy,* Eerdmans, 1954, p. 27.
5. P. E. Burroughs, The Sunday School Board of the Southern Baptist Convention, 1928 (Foreword).
6. Carl W. Werner, Sr., *The Power of Pure Stewardship,* Concordia, 1970, p. 39.
7. Fleming H. Revell, 1938, p. 8.

Chapter 3

1. *The Message of Stewardship,* Abingdon-Cokesbury, 1922, p. 33.
2. Henry H. Halley, *Bible Handbook,* p. 59.
3. Charles J. Burton, *The Mathematics of the Sky,* Standard Press, 1920.
4. Mt. 18:10; Is. 6:3; Ps. 103:2; Gen. 3:11.
5. Dan. 8:16, 17; Mt. 2:13; Lk. 19:20; Acts 5:19, 20; Rev. 1:1.
6. Mt. 13:39; 16:27; 25:21; 1 Thess. 1:7.
7. Eph. 1:10; Rev. 5:13; 7:9-12.

Chapter 4

1. Col. 3:10; Eph. 4:24.
2. *The Concept of the Believers' Church,* Herald Press, 1969.
3. Deut. 4:12; Jer. 11:4.
4. Ex. 7:16; 8:1; 9:13.
5. Col. 1:20; Eph. 1:20.

Chapter 5

1. Is. 49:13; see also Ps. 148:3-10.
2. Byfield and Shaw, *Your Money and Your God,* Doubleday, 1959, p. 33.
3. 1 Cor. 9:16, 22.

Chapter 6

1. William Barclay, *Word Books,* 1971, p. 261 (used with permission).
2. *Ibid.,* 278 f.
3. *Stewardship Vitalized,* Sunday School Board of the Southern Baptist Convention, Nashville, 1926, pp. 18 f.
4. *Ibid.,* p. 4.

Chapter 7

1. Ps. 50:3; 65:17-25; Dan. 7:10, 11; Rom. 8:19-23; 2 Cor. 5:19; Eph. 1:10; Col. 1:20; 2 Pet. 3:4; Rev. 21:1.
2. H. Barnette, *The Church and the Ecological Crisis,* Eerdmans, 1972, p. 14.
3. *Ibid.,* p. 23.
4. Steward L. Udall, *The Quiet Crisis,* Holt, Rinehart, and Winston, 1963.
5. *Ibid.*

6. Charles M. Crow, *Stewardship Sermons*, Abingdon Press, 1960, pp. 12 f. (used with permission).

7. William N. Oatis, Associated Press, Newton, Kansas.

8. *Pollution and the Death of Man*, Tyndale, 1970, p. 65.

9. Robert Rienow, and Leona Train, *Moment in the Sun*, Ballantine Books, 1967, p. 217.

10. *Christianity Today*, September 15, 1972.

11. *Op. cit.*, p. 32.

12. *Ibid.*, p. 90.

Chapter 9

1. Doubleday, 1959, p. 43.

2. Deut. 12:5-7; 14:22-27.

Chapter 10

1. Earl V. Pierce, *The Supreme Beatitude*, Fleming H. Revell Co., 1947, p. 30.

2. Carl Henry, *Christian Personal Ethics*, Eerdmans, 1957, p. 546.

3. John M. Versteeg, *When Christ Controls*, Abingdon-Cokesbury, 1943, p. 117.

4. *The Christian and His Money Problems*, George Doran Co., 1923, p. 105.

Chapter 12

1. Tobit 1:6-8.

2. *Complete Works of Josephus*, p. 111.

3. Mal. 3:7, 8, *The Living Bible*.

4. Mt. 23:23, TEV.

5. Dr. William Smith and Professor Cheetham, *Dictionary of Antiquities*, Vol. II, p. 1963.

6. *Ante-Nicene Fathers*, Vol. VII, p. 471.

7. *The Encyclopedia Americana*.

8. Elsie Stapleton, *Spending for Happiness*, Prentice-Hall Inc., Englewood Cliffs, N.J., 1949 (used with permission).

9. William Weekly, *Getting and Giving*, United Brethren Publishing House, 1963, pp. 43 f.

10. Raymond E. Balcomb, *Stir What You've Got*, Abingdon Press, 1968, pp. 28 f. (used with permission).

11. Lettie B. Cowman, *Charles Cowman*, Oriental Missionary Society, 1928, p. 80.

12. Pierce, *op. cit.*, p. 33.

13. Ernest G. Thomas, *Spiritual Life Through Tithing*, Tidings, 1953, pp. 36, 55.

14. Grindstaff, *Developing a Giving Church*, Fleming H. Revell, 1944, pp. 13, 14.

Chapter 13

1. LeTourneau, *NOW*, October, 1972.

2. Irving, *Master of Money*, Fleming H. Revell, 1936, p. 54.

3. Simpson, *Into My Storehouse*, Fleming H. Revell, 1940, p. 78.

4. Robert Stover, San Francisco, *Wichita Eagle*, March 9, 1973.

5. Lettie B. Cowman, *Charles Cowman*, Oriental Missionary Society, 1928.

THE AUTHOR

Milo Kauffman was born February 13, 1898, near Harrisonville, Mo. He spent his boyhood years on a farm in North Dakota. He received the BA degree from Hesston College, the BD from Northern Baptist Theological Seminary, the MA from McCormick, and the STD from Pikes Peak Seminary.

From 1932 to 1951 he was president of Hesston College, Hesston, Kansas, and since that time has served intermittently on the faculty. He was asked to prepare the Conrad Grebel Lectures in 1953 on Christian stewardship. These lectures were published as *The Challenge of Christian Stewardship*. The book went through five printings and enjoyed a wide acceptance. In 1962 Kauffman was asked by the Mennonite Board of Missions to deliver the lectures to churches and Christian groups in India and Japan.

Kauffman was ordained to the ministry in 1924 and has held pastorates in Kansas and Illinois. He has served widely in evangelistic meetings and Bible conferences, as well as on church boards and committees.